SHARE MARKET EXPERT

THE TRUTH ABOUT TRADING

ANKIT KUMAR

Made with ♥ on the Notion Press Platform
www.notionpress.com

This Book I specially dedicate to My Father Mr. Ashok Singh and My mother Mrs. Rinku Devi . I want to thank my mother and father who made me worthy that today I have seen this world, I want to thank my friends who gave me a lot of good things in my life. I also want to pay tribute to the God who given konwledge and Power to me for write this Book. Thank to all for everything.

Ankit Kumar

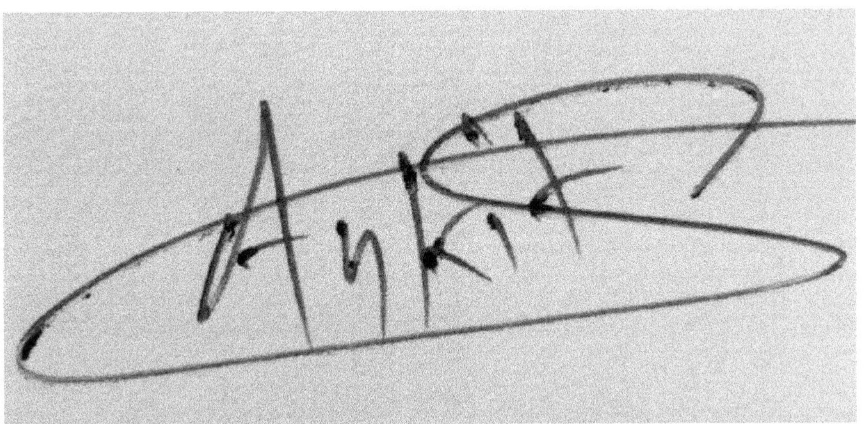

Enter Caption

Contents

Acknowledgements

The stock market is a complex and important part of the global economy. It plays a vital role in the allocation of capital and resources, allowing businesses to raise funds for expansion and investment, and providing individuals with the opportunity to invest and grow their wealth.

While the stock market can be a source of financial opportunity and growth, it can also be volatile and unpredictable. It is important to acknowledge the risks associated with investing in the stock market, and to carefully consider one's investment goals, risk tolerance, and financial situation before making any investment decisions.

In addition, it is important to recognize that the stock market is influenced by a variety of factors, including economic indicators, company earnings reports, geopolitical events, and investor sentiment. It is important to stay informed and up-to-date on these factors in order to make informed investment decisions and manage risk effectively.

Introduction

Stock is the general term that is used to describe the ownership of the company. Stocks can be bought and sold on the exchanges through a broker. Owning the stock of a particular company gives you the right to vote in the shareholder's meeting, get the dividend when and if it is declared. Your voting power increases if you own the majority of the stocks of a particular company. In short, you can indirectly control the company by choosing its board of directors.

The Stock market is the place where you can buy or sell the shares of the companies which are listed on the exchanges.In simple words, when you need groceries, you go to the local supermarket in the same way when you are willing to invest in stocks or mutual funds you usually buy them through the stock market. Stock markets can be also called equity markets or share markets. The one who buys the stock of the company is called a buyer and the one who sells the stock of the company is called the seller.

Market participants :Many large and well-known companies have been listed on the stock exchanges. Along with stocks, bonds and derivatives are also traded on the stock exchanges. Participants in the share market range from small individual stock investors to larger investors. Small investors are called retail investors and large investors are called high net worth investors. Along with individuals' different institutions and corporations can also invest or trade on the stock exchanges.

The Indian institutions who invest or trade on the stock exchanges are referred to as Domestic Institutional Investors (DII's) and the foreign institutions who invest or trade on Indian exchanges are referred to as Foreign Institutional Investors (FII's).

In this Book all Termilogy of Systematic investing Explained so the New trader can take important decisions related trdading and can book profit behalf of these strategies.

CHAPTER ONE

Share Market

The share market, also known as the stock market or equity market, is a platform where publicly traded companies sell their shares to investors. When a company wants to raise capital, they can do so by issuing shares, which represent ownership in the company. Investors can buy these shares, which gives them a stake in the company's profits and assets.

Companies list their stock through a process (initial public offering or IPO) and investors purchase those shares. Which allows the company to raise money to grow its business. Investors then buy and sell these shares whereas exchange keeps the track of demand and supply of each listed stock. Buyers offer a "bid," ie. The highest amount they're willing to pay. Which is usually lesser than the amount, sellers "ask" for in exchange. This difference is called the bid-ask spread. Computers often do the calculations, with the help of algorithms. To determine how much participants are willing to buy or sell..

The share market provides a way for companies to raise capital, and for investors to buy and sell shares of these companies. Investors can make money by buying shares at a low price and selling them at a higher price. The share market is regulated by government agencies, such as the Securities and Exchange of India (SEBI) in the India, to ensure transparency and fairness in trading. It is also important to note that investing in the share market comes with risks, and investors should do their due diligence before making any investments.

How is the price of the stock decided?

The price of the stock is decided based on supply and demand. There are always two groups in the market. One group is referred to as buyers, one who buys the stock, and another group is referred to as sellers, one who sells the shares. A potential buyer bids a specific price for a stock, and a potential seller asks a specific price for the same stock. When bid price and ask price matches, trade takes place on a first-come, first-served basis if there is more than one bidder at a given price. In this way, the price of the stock is decided. If the number of buyers is greater than the number of sellers, the price of the stock increases as the seller tends to sell costlier. When the number of sellers is greater than the number of buyers, the price of the stock tends to decrease. I hope that, in today's blog of beginner's guide to the stock market,

History of share market in india :

The history of share market in India dates back to the mid-19th century during the British colonial rule. The first organized stock exchange in India was established in 1875, called the Bombay Stock Exchange (BSE). Initially, the BSE dealt mainly in cotton and bullion, but over time it expanded to include other commodities and securities.

The Calcutta Stock Exchange was founded in 1908 and became the second stock exchange in India. In 1957, the Delhi Stock Exchange was established, followed by the Madras Stock Exchange in 1937.

After India gained independence in 1947, the Indian stock market started to grow rapidly. In 1992, the Indian government initiated economic reforms, which led to the liberalization of the stock market and the opening up of the economy to foreign investment.

In 1994, the National Stock Exchange (NSE) was established, which introduced electronic trading and became the first exchange in India to offer a fully automated trading system. The NSE became the largest stock exchange in India, surpassing the BSE in terms of trading volume.

In recent years, the Indian stock market has continued to grow and evolve, with the introduction of new financial products such as exchange-traded funds (ETFs) and the launch of new stock exchanges. Today, India has two major stock exchanges, the BSE and the NSE, and several regional exchanges operating in different parts of the country. The Indian stock market has become an important component of the country's economy, providing a platform for companies to raise capital and for investors to participate in the growth of the Indian economy.

Share :

A share, also known as a stock or equity, is a unit of ownership in a company. When a company wants to raise capital, they can issue shares, which represent a portion of ownership in the company. Each share represents a fraction of the company's assets, earnings, and voting rights.

When an investor buys a share, they become a shareholder in the company and have a claim on a portion of the company's profits and assets. Shareholders can benefit from their investment through dividends, which are a portion of the company's profits paid out to shareholders, or by selling their shares at a higher price than they purchased them for.

Shares are bought and sold on the share market, where investors can trade shares with one another. The price of shares is determined by supply and demand, with more demand for a company's shares driving up the price, and vice versa. Shares can be a way for investors to grow their wealth, but they come with risks and investors should do their due diligence before making any investments.

- The market Of Finance
- Stocks & IPOs
- Futures & Options
- Mutual funds & ETFs
- Currency & Commodity
- Algotrading
- Global Investing

Stocks :

A stock, also known as a share or equity, represents a unit of ownership in a publicly-traded company. When a company wants to raise money, it can issue stocks to investors, who then become partial owners of the company.

The value of a stock can go up or down based on a variety of factors, including the performance of the company, market conditions, and investor sentiment. Investors can buy and sell stocks on stock exchanges, with the price of a stock fluctuating based on supply and demand.

Owning stocks can provide investors with potential capital appreciation and income in the form of dividends. However, stocks also carry risks, and the value of a stock can decrease, potentially resulting in losses for the investor.

IPO :

IPO stands for Initial Public Offering. It refers to the process of a private company going public by selling its shares of stock to the public for the first time.

In an IPO, the company typically works with an investment bank or underwriter to determine the offering price, the number of shares to be sold, and the timing of the offering. The underwriter also helps the company navigate the regulatory requirements of going public, such as filing a registration statement with the Securities and Exchange of India

Once the IPO is completed, the company's shares will be listed on a stock exchange, such as the National Stock Exchange or BSE, where they can be bought and sold by investors. The funds raised from the IPO can be used by the company for various purposes, such as expanding the business, paying off debt, or investing in research and development.

Futures & Options :

Futures and options are financial instruments used by traders and investors to manage risk or speculate on price movements in financial markets.

Futures contracts are agreements to buy or sell a specific asset (such as a commodity, currency, or stock index) at a predetermined price and date in the future. The buyer of a futures contract agrees to purchase the underlying asset at the agreed-upon price on the specified future date, while the seller of the contract agrees to sell the asset at that price. Futures contracts are standardized and traded on organized exchanges, with the exchange acting as the counterparty to every trade.

Options contracts, on the other hand, give the holder the right, but not the obligation, to buy or sell an underlying asset at a predetermined price and date in the future. There are two types of options: call options and put options. A call option gives the holder the right to buy the underlying asset, while a put option gives the holder the right to sell the underlying asset. Options are traded on exchanges and can be used for hedging or speculation.

Both futures and options can be used for hedging, where an investor takes a position in the derivative contract to offset potential losses in another asset. They can also be used for speculation, where an investor takes a position in the derivative contract in the hopes of making a profit from price movements in the underlying asset. However, futures contracts carry more risk than options, as the buyer of a futures contract is obligated to buy or sell the underlying asset at the agreed-upon price on the specified future date, regardless of the market price at that time.

Mutual funds & ETFs :

Mutual funds and ETFs (Exchange-Traded Funds) are both investment vehicles that allow individuals to invest in a diversified portfolio of stocks, bonds, and other assets, without having to buy individual securities.

Mutual funds are pools of money that are managed by professional portfolio managers who invest the money in a diversified portfolio of stocks, bonds, and other assets. Investors buy shares in the mutual fund, and the value of their investment is determined by the performance of the underlying portfolio. Mutual funds are typically bought and sold through a fund company, and their prices are set at the end of each trading day.

ETFs, on the other hand, are similar to mutual funds in that they also hold a diversified portfolio of securities. However, ETFs are traded on an exchange like stocks, and their prices fluctuate throughout the trading day. ETFs are often preferred by investors who want the flexibility to trade throughout the day, and they may also have lower expense ratios than mutual funds.

Both mutual funds and ETFs offer investors a way to diversify their investments across a range of asset classes, sectors, and geographies. However, it's important to research and compare the fees, performance history, and investment strategies of each fund before making an investment decision.

Currency & Commodity :

Currency and commodity are two different types of assets that are traded in financial markets.

Currency refers to the form of money that is used as a medium of exchange for goods and services. Examples of currencies include the US dollar, the euro, the Japanese yen, and the British pound. Currency trading involves buying and selling currencies in pairs, such as USD/EUR or USD/JPY. The foreign exchange (forex) market is the largest financial market in the world and is where most currency trading takes place.

Commodity refers to a raw material or primary agricultural product that can be bought and sold, such as gold, oil, wheat, coffee, or sugar. Commodity trading involves buying and selling commodities with the aim of making a profit. Commodity markets are typically divided into two categories: hard commodities, which are natural resources that must be mined or extracted, and soft commodities, which are agricultural products that must be grown.

Both currency and commodity trading can be highly volatile and subject to market fluctuations. Traders use a variety of strategies and techniques to analyze market trends and make trading decisions, such as technical analysis, fundamental analysis, and news-based analysis.

Algotrading :

Algotrading, also known as algorithmic trading or automated trading, is the use of computer algorithms to execute trades in financial markets. It involves using computer programs and mathematical models to analyze market data and make trading decisions, without the need for human intervention.

Algotrading systems can be used to execute a wide range of trading strategies, including trend following, mean reversion, statistical arbitrage, and high-frequency trading. These systems can analyze vast amounts of data, such as price and volume data, news releases, and social media sentiment, to identify trading opportunities and execute trades at high speeds.

Algotrading has become increasingly popular in recent years, with many institutional and individual investors using automated trading systems to improve their trading performance. However, it also comes with certain risks, such as system failures, errors in programming, and the possibility of unexpected market events. As such, it is important for traders to carefully design and test their algorithms, and to implement risk management strategies to minimize potential losses.

Global Investing :

Global investing refers to the practice of investing in securities or assets from companies located in different countries around the world. It is a popular strategy for diversifying investment portfolios and mitigating risk, as it allows investors to spread their investments across different economies and industries.

There are many different types of global investments, including stocks, bonds, mutual funds, exchange-traded funds (ETFs), and real estate investment trusts (REITs). Global investors may also choose to invest directly in foreign currencies or in commodities like gold and oil.

Global investing requires a deep understanding of different markets, economies, and political landscapes. Factors such as currency fluctuations, geopolitical risks, and differences in regulations and taxation can all impact the success of a global investment. As such, global investors often rely on extensive research and analysis to make informed investment decisions.

Demat Account :

Demat or Dematerialization is the process of converting physical share certificates into electronic form. In other words, demat refers to the process of holding securities such as stocks, bonds, mutual funds, etc. in an electronic form, eliminating the need for physical certificates. The process of dematerialization is facilitated by a depository, which holds the electronic securities on behalf of the investors.

The demat account, which is similar to a bank account, is used to hold the electronic securities. The demat account provides a convenient and secure way for investors to buy, sell, and transfer securities. It eliminates the need for investors to keep physical certificates, which can be lost, stolen, or damaged.

Demat accounts are mandatory in India for trading in securities in the stock market. In many other countries, the process of dematerialization is also widely used, and investors are encouraged to hold their securities in electronic form.

Trading :

Trading refers to the buying and selling of financial assets, such as stocks, bonds, currencies, commodities, and derivatives, with the aim of making a profit. Trading can be done through various platforms and methods, including online trading platforms, brokerages, and trading desks.

To trade, you need to follow a few basic steps:

Choose a trading platform or brokerage: There are numerous trading platforms and brokerages available, and you need to choose one that suits your trading style, budget, and requirements.

Open an account: Once you've selected a trading platform or brokerage, you need to open an account. This usually involves providing personal information and completing the necessary documentation.

Fund your account: You need to deposit funds into your trading account before you can start trading. The amount you need to deposit depends on the trading platform or brokerage you choose.

Choose a financial asset to trade: You need to select the financial asset you want to trade. This could be stocks, currencies, commodities, or derivatives.

Analyze the market: Before making a trade, you need to analyze the market and determine whether the asset's value is likely to rise or fall.

Place your trade: Once you've decided to trade, you need to place your order. You can choose to buy or sell the asset, and you can also set parameters, such as stop-loss and take-profit levels.

Monitor your trade: Once your trade is open, you need to monitor it to see how it's performing. You can also adjust your parameters as necessary.

Close your trade: You can close your trade at any time, either by taking your profit or cutting your losses.

It's important to note that trading involves risks, and it's essential to educate yourself about the market, trading strategies, and risk management techniques before you start trading. It's also advisable to start with a small amount of capital and gradually increase it as you gain experience and confidence.

Biggest market crash of world :

There have been several significant market crashes throughout history, but the biggest market crash in modern times was the 1929 stock market crash, also known as the Great Crash or Black Tuesday.

The crash began on October 24, 1929, when the New York Stock Exchange experienced a sudden and massive sell-off. This led to a panic among investors, causing stock prices to plummet further. The market continued to decline over the following weeks, with Black Tuesday on October 29, 1929, marking the most devastating day of the crash.

The crash was triggered by a combination of factors, including speculation, overproduction, and the widespread use of credit to purchase stocks. The resulting economic downturn, known as the Great Depression, lasted for several years and had a profound impact on the global economy, leading to widespread poverty, unemployment, and social unrest.

Since then, there have been other notable market crashes, including the 1987 Black Monday crash, the Dotcom bubble burst in 2000, and the 2008 financial crisis, but none have had the same level of global impact as the 1929 crash.

Scam of the world :

Indias biggest stock market scam

One of India's biggest stock market scams was the Harshad Mehta scam, which occurred in the early 1990s. Harshad Mehta was a stockbroker who manipulated the stock market by exploiting loopholes in the banking system.

Mehta took advantage of the ready forward (RF) deals, a type of loan given by banks to brokers against government securities. He used this money to buy shares in large quantities, creating an artificial demand and driving up the stock prices. He also used a technique called circular trading, in which he bought and sold shares among a group of brokers to manipulate prices.

The scam was exposed when the Reserve Bank of India tightened regulations on RF deals, causing Mehta's schemes to unravel. The scam led to a crash in the stock market, and Mehta was arrested and charged with fraud and cheating.

The scam caused losses of around Rs 4,000 crore (equivalent to approximately $800 million at the time) and highlighted the need for stronger regulations in India's financial system. The Securities and Exchange Board of India (SEBI) was established in the aftermath of the scam to regulate the securities market and prevent similar incidents from occurring in the future.

Wall of street scam One of the most well-known stock market scams in the United States is the Wall Street scam perpetrated by Jordan Belfort, also known as the "Wolf of Wall Street."

Belfort was a stockbroker who founded a firm called Stratton Oakmont in the late 1980s. He and his team of brokers engaged in a scheme known as "pump and dump," in which they would manipulate the prices of penny stocks by artificially inflating their value through false and misleading statements. They would then sell the stocks at the higher price, leaving unsuspecting investors with worthless shares.

Belfort and his associates also engaged in other fraudulent activities, such as charging exorbitant fees and making unauthorized trades in clients' accounts. They used the proceeds from these activities to fund a lavish lifestyle that included drugs, prostitutes, and luxury cars and homes.

The scam eventually came to light, and Belfort was arrested and charged with securities fraud and money laundering. He pleaded guilty and served time in prison, and was also ordered to pay restitution to the victims of his scam.

The Wall Street scam was the subject of a bestselling book by Belfort, as well as a Hollywood movie directed by Martin Scorsese and starring Leonardo DiCaprio as Belfort. The scandal highlighted the need for stronger regulations and enforcement in the financial industry to protect investors from fraudulent activities.

What is a Demat Account?

A Demat account is nothing but a dematerialized account used to store financial securities such as stocks, bonds, etc. in electronic form. In India, Demat accounts are maintained by two depository organizations named National Securities Depository Limited (NSDL) and Central Depository Services Limited (CDSL).

Mainly there are three types of Demat account-

Regular Demat Account

Regular Demat account is for the Indian residents who are willing to hold the securities.

Repatriable Demat Account

This account is for non-resident Indians, those who want to invest in Indian securities. This type of Demat account requires an NRE (Non-Resident External) bank account associated with it.

Non-Repatriable Demat Account

This account is for non-resident Indians but this type of Demat account requires an NRO (Non-Resident Ordinary) account associated with it.

What is a Trading Account?

If you are willing to invest in the stock market then it is not possible to directly connect with the exchange and buy the shares. First, you have to open an account with the broker, and through the broker you can buy or sell the securities. The account which you open with the broker for buying and selling securities is called a trading account.

There are different types of brokers such as-

Service Brokers

Discount Brokers

Service brokers provide a wide range of services for their clients that includes buying/selling of shares, stock research, stock buy/sell recommendation, etc. For this, they charge more than the discount broker.

Discount brokers only provide trading services to their clients. That is why they charge less than service brokers. Zerodha and UpStox are India's best discount brokers. The interfaces of Zerodha and Upstox are very user-friendly, and you can buy/sell the shares through them very easily.

Steps To Open A Demat Account Online

1. Choose Your Broker – This is the first and very important step while opening a trading and Demat account. You need to open your Demat account as well. For this purpose, you should choose a SEBI registered broker having a valid registration number issued by SEBI.
2. Visit The Broker's Website – After selecting the broker, visit the official website of that broker and register yourself by using your phone number. (Make sure that your phone number has been linked to your Aadhar.)
3. Fill In The Necessary Details – After the successful registration, the broker will ask you to fill in the primary information like your Email Id, PAN Number, Aadhar Number, Occupation, Date of Birth, etc.

4. Upload The Required Documents – After filling in the required information, you have to submit the following documents-

   PAN card
   Aadhar card
   Canceled Cheque/Bank Passbook/Bank statement (1 month)
   Your signature on white paper
   Income proof (optional – if you want to trade in F&O)

5. Link Bank Account – After uploading these documents, you have to fill in your bank account details.
6. In-Person Verification- In-person verification is the mandatory step according to the rules and regulations of the SEBI. In this step, the broker will give you an OTP, and you have to write down that OTP on paper, and you have to hold that paper in front of your webcam.
7. E-Sign The Application Form – After completing the in-person verification it will ask you to e-sign the application form. Once your email verification is done, you will be redirected to the NSDL page on which you have to provide a 12-digit Aadhar number. After that, confirm the OTP that will be sent to you through your Aadhar registered mobile number.

Once you are done with this, the application form will automatically open in front of you along with the e-sign option. Once you click the e-sign option the process of account opening for the equity segment will be completed. If you have chosen the commodity segment also in that case, you have to repeat this step.

8. Get Your Client ID And Password- This completes the process of opening the trading and Demat account. You will receive your login credentials and client ID through the mail after verification of the provided documents. The mail will also contain some instructions regarding how to log in and use the broker's app.

Key Notes :

- **Share Market is Risky, knowledge is very important before Trading in Stock Market.**

- Don't take it as a gambling, Deal it as a Business.
- There is lot of humour in Market and Manupulation so dont hurry to invest in any stock
- watch Gloabal Market, National Market, Govt Anouncements, Sectors Commodities & Companies news
- Check Pre Market and open market and check the results of the stock and practice.

CHAPTER TWO

Financial Education

Finance :

Finance refers to the management of money, investments, and other financial instruments. It encompasses a wide range of activities related to the acquisition, allocation, and management of financial resources. Finance involves making decisions about how to raise capital, how to invest funds, and how to manage financial risks.

Finance is important for individuals, businesses, and governments alike. Individuals need to manage their personal finances to achieve financial security and stability. Businesses require finance to fund their operations, invest in new projects, and manage financial risks. Governments use finance to manage public spending, regulate financial markets, and ensure economic stability.

Finance includes various sub-disciplines, such as corporate finance, investment management, financial planning, risk management, and financial accounting. Each of these areas of finance focuses on different aspects of managing money and financial resources.

Financial education help in managing income :

Financial education can help in managing income in several ways:

- **Budgeting**: Financial education can teach individuals how to create a budget that outlines their income and expenses. By understanding where their money is going, individuals can identify areas where they can cut back on expenses and save more money.
- **Setting financial goals:** With financial education, individuals can learn how to set financial goals, such as saving for retirement, buying a house, or paying off debt. Setting clear financial goals can help individuals prioritize their spending and make informed decisions about how to allocate their income.

- **Understanding debt:** Financial education can help individuals understand the different types of debt, such as credit card debt, student loans, and mortgages. By understanding the impact of interest rates and the importance of making timely payments, individuals can avoid falling into debt traps and manage their debt effectively.
- **Investing**: Financial education can teach individuals about investing in different types of assets, such as stocks, bonds, and mutual funds. By understanding the potential risks and rewards of different investment strategies, individuals can make informed decisions about how to grow their wealth.

Savings :

Savings refer to the portion of one's income or money that is set aside and not spent immediately, with the intention of using it for a future purpose. Savings can take many forms, including money deposited into a savings account, investments in stocks, bonds, or real estate, or physical assets such as gold or property.

The act of saving money is an important financial habit that can help individuals and households achieve their financial goals and improve their overall financial health. Saving money can be used to build an emergency fund, pay for large purchases, such as a home or car, or invest in retirement or other long-term financial goals.

Savings can also provide a sense of financial security, as having a savings cushion can help individuals and households weather unexpected financial setbacks, such as job loss, illness, or unexpected expenses.

Investments :

Investments refer to the allocation of resources, such as money or time, with the expectation of generating some return or profit in the future. The objective of investing is to increase the value of the investment over time or generate a steady stream of income.

There are various types of investments, including stocks, bonds, mutual funds, real estate, commodities, and alternative investments like private equity and hedge funds. The risk and potential return associated with each investment vary, and investors must assess their risk tolerance and investment goals before choosing which type of investment to pursue.

Investments can be made by individuals, corporations, governments, or other organizations. The primary reasons for investing include building wealth, earning income, funding retirement, and achieving financial goals.

Successful investing requires knowledge, research, and a long-term perspective, as the value of investments can fluctuate over time.

Steps in Investing Planning Process :

The steps involved in the investing planning process are as follows:

- **Define your investment goals**: Start by identifying your investment goals and objectives. This could include short-term goals such as saving for a vacation or long-term goals such as retirement planning.
- **Assess your risk tolerance**: Determine your risk tolerance by assessing your financial situation, investment experience, and personal preferences. This will help you determine the appropriate level of risk for your investment portfolio.
- **Develop an investment strategy**: Based on your goals and risk tolerance, develop an investment strategy that aligns with your investment objectives. This could include selecting specific investment vehicles such as stocks, bonds, mutual funds, ETFs, real estate, or a combination of these.
- **Allocate your assets**: Determine how to allocate your assets across your investment portfolio. This will depend on your investment strategy, risk tolerance, and the investment vehicles you choose. Diversification is key to reducing risk.
- **Implement your investment plan**: Once you have developed an investment plan, it's time to implement it. This could involve opening an investment account, selecting investment vehicles, and placing trades.
- **Monitor and adjust your portfolio**: Monitor your investment portfolio regularly to ensure it's on track to meet your goals. Make adjustments as needed to maintain your desired asset allocation and risk level.
- **Re-evaluate your investment plan**: Finally, periodically re-evaluate your investment plan to ensure it's still aligned with your goals and objectives. As your financial situation and goals change over time, your investment plan may need to be adjusted accordingly.

Diversify Investment :

Diversifying investments is important for several reasons:

- **Mitigating Risk**: Diversification helps to spread your investments across different assets, industries, and markets, which reduces the overall risk of your portfolio. If you put all your money in one asset or market, you are exposed to a higher level of risk, and if that asset or market performs poorly, you stand to lose a lot of money. Diversifying helps to mitigate this risk by spreading your investments across different areas, so that if one area performs poorly, you still have other investments that may perform well.

- **Maximizing Returns:** By diversifying your investments, you can potentially maximize your returns. Different assets and markets perform differently at different times. By investing in a variety of assets, you increase your chances of investing in an area that is performing well, while also reducing your risk.
- **Providing Flexibility**: Diversification provides flexibility in your investment strategy. If you have all your money invested in one asset or market, it may be difficult to make changes to your investments if market conditions change. By diversifying, you can adjust your investments as needed, depending on market conditions, without having to completely sell off one type of investment.
- **Reducing Emotional Investing**: Diversification can help to reduce emotional investing. If you have all your money invested in one asset or market, you may be more likely to make emotional decisions based on short-term market fluctuations. By diversifying, you can take a more long-term view of your investments and avoid making rash decisions based on short-term market movements.
- **Budgeting :**
- Budgeting is the process of creating a financial plan that outlines an individual's or an organization's expected income and expenses for a specific period, usually for a month, a quarter, or a year. The primary goal of budgeting is to help individuals or organizations to manage their money efficiently, make informed financial decisions, and ensure that their expenses do not exceed their income.
- Budgeting involves identifying all sources of income, such as salaries, investments, and rental income, and all expenses, such as rent, utilities, groceries, entertainment, and other bills. Once all the income and expenses are identified, individuals or organizations can allocate their funds appropriately to ensure that they have enough money to cover their essential expenses and save for future goals.
- Creating a budget can be a useful tool in managing finances, tracking spending habits, and making informed financial decisions. It helps individuals and organizations to stay on track financially and avoid

overspending, accumulating debt, or living beyond their means.

The budgeting process involves several steps that organizations typically follow to create and manage a budget. These steps include:

1. **Establish goals and objectives:** The first step in the budgeting process is to identify the organization's goals and objectives. These goals may include increasing revenue, reducing expenses, investing in new projects, or improving profitability.
2. **Gather financial data:** Next, the organization needs to collect financial data to inform the budgeting process. This may include historical financial statements, sales data, expense reports, and projections for future revenue and expenses.
3. **Develop a budget plan**: Using the financial data collected, the organization can begin to develop a budget plan. This plan should include estimates of revenue and expenses for the upcoming period, typically a year.
4. **Review and revise**: Once the budget plan is developed, it should be reviewed and revised as needed. This may involve consulting with various departments or stakeholders to ensure that the budget aligns with their goals and priorities.
5. **Obtain approval:** Once the budget plan is finalized, it should be presented to the appropriate stakeholders for approval. This may include the board of directors, executive team, or other key decision-makers.
6. **Implement and monitor**: After the budget plan is approved, the organization can begin to implement it. Throughout the year, the organization should monitor actual performance against the budget plan and make adjustments as needed to stay on track.
7. **Evaluate and adjust**: At the end of the budget period, the organization should evaluate its performance and adjust the budget plan as necessary for the upcoming period.
8. Overall, the budgeting process is a dynamic and ongoing process that requires ongoing monitoring and adjustment to ensure that the organization is on track to meet its goals and objectives.

Household Finances :

Household finances refer to the management of money and resources within a household or family unit. This includes budgeting, saving, investing, and spending money on various household expenses, such as housing, utilities, groceries, and transportation. Effective management of household finances is important to ensure financial stability and security for the family.

Some key aspects of household finances include creating and sticking to a budget, saving for emergencies and long-term goals, reducing debt, and investing for the future. It is also important to have open communication and transparency about finances within the family unit to ensure that everyone is on the same page and working towards common goals.

Here are some steps for maintaining household finances:

- **Create a budget**: A budget is an essential tool for managing household finances. It allows you to see how much money is coming in and going out each month. You can use a budgeting app or a spreadsheet to create your budget.
- **Track your spending**: Keeping track of your spending helps you stay within your budget. You can use a spending tracker app or keep receipts to help you keep track of your expenses.
- **Pay bills on time**: Late fees can quickly add up and hurt your financial situation. Make sure to pay your bills on time each month, or set up automatic payments to avoid late fees.
- **Set financial goals**: Setting financial goals can help you stay motivated and focused on your long-term financial objectives. Whether it's paying off debt or saving for a down payment on a house, having clear goals can help you stay on track.
- **Build an emergency fund**: An emergency fund is money set aside for unexpected expenses, such as a medical emergency or car repair. Aim to save three to six months‘ worth of living expenses in your emergency fund.
- **Reduce debt:** High-interest debt can be a major obstacle to achieving your financial goals. Consider paying off debt with the highest interest rates first, or look into debt consolidation options.

Save for retirement: Saving for retirement is essential, even if it feels far off. Consider contributing to a 401(k) or IRA to ensure that you have enough money saved for retirement.

Review your finances regularly: Regularly reviewing your finances can help you identify areas where you can cut back or make improvements.

Make a habit of reviewing your budget and expenses monthly or quarterly to stay on top of your finances.

Goals of Fundamental Analysis : To determine the fair value of a Company.

Qualitative factors which affect stock investing :

Stock investing involves a wide range of factors that can influence the value of a company and its stock price. In addition to quantitative factors such as financial statements and market trends, there are also several qualitative factors that can affect stock investing. Here are some examples:

Management Quality: The quality of a company's management team can have a significant impact on its stock price. Investors may look for factors such as experience, track record, and transparency when evaluating a management team.

Brand Reputation: A strong brand reputation & Business Model can lead to customer loyalty, higher sales, and increased profitability. Companies with strong brand recognition and a positive reputation may be more attractive to investors.

Competitive Advantage: The competitive Advantage within an industry can have a significant impact on a company's stock price. Companies that are able to stay ahead of their competitors may be more likely to succeed in the long run.

Regulatory Environment: The regulatory environment in which a company operates can affect its stock price. Changes in regulations or the introduction of new regulations can have a positive or negative impact on a company's profitability.

Industry Trends: The overall trends within an industry can also have an impact on stock investing. For example, an industry that is growing rapidly may attract more investment, while an industry in decline may be less attractive.

Social and Environmental Factors: Investors are increasingly looking at companies' social and environmental practices when making investment decisions. Companies that are seen as socially responsible and environmentally conscious may be more attractive to investors.

Investor Sentiment: Investor sentiment, or how investors feel about a particular company or the market as a whole, can also affect stock prices. Positive sentiment can drive prices up, while negative sentiment can drive prices down.

Overall, qualitative factors can be just as important as quantitative factors Corporate governance , ownership & Insider Slaes , Digital Marketing when it comes to stock investing. Investors need to consider both types of factors when evaluating potential investments.

Quantitative factors which affect stock price :

Quantitative factors are objective and measurable financial metrics that can have a direct impact on the stock price of a company. Some of the most important quantitative factors that can affect stock price include:

Revenue and Earnings: The revenue and earnings of a company are among the most important quantitative factors affecting stock price. If a company reports higher than expected revenue and earnings, its stock price is likely to rise, and vice versa.

Profit Margins: Profit margins are a measure of a company's profitability. Higher profit margins generally indicate a stronger financial position and can lead to a higher stock price.

Valuation Ratios: Valuation ratios such as price-to-earnings (P/E) ratio, price-to-sales (P/S) ratio, and price-to-book (P/B) ratio can also affect stock price. A company with a higher P/E ratio is typically viewed as having higher growth potential, while a company with a lower P/E ratio is viewed as being undervalued.

Dividend Yield: The dividend yield is the annual dividend payment divided by the stock price. Companies that pay higher dividends tend to be viewed as less risky and more attractive to investors, which can lead to a higher stock price.

Market Trends: Market trends, such as interest rates and inflation, can also have an impact on stock prices. Higher interest rates can lead to lower stock prices, while lower interest rates can lead to higher stock prices.

Economic Indicators: Economic indicators, such as gross domestic product (GDP), unemployment rates, and consumer price index (CPI), can also affect stock prices. Positive economic indicators generally lead to higher stock prices, while negative indicators can lead to lower stock prices.

Analyst Recommendations: Analyst recommendations, such as buy, hold, or sell, can also affect stock prices. Positive recommendations from analysts can lead to higher stock prices, while negative recommendations can lead to lower stock prices.

Overall, quantitative factors provide investors with a way to measure a company's financial health and performance. By analyzing these factors Market Share,Industry Growth,Customer,Competition, investors can make more informed investment decisions.

Importance of financial statement in trading :

Financial statements are an essential tool for traders as they provide crucial information about a company's financial performance and position. The three primary financial statements are the income statement, balance sheet, and cash flow statement.

Income Statement: It provides information about a company's revenues, expenses, and net income over a specific period. It helps traders to evaluate the profitability of a company and its ability to generate consistent earnings.

Balance Sheet: It shows a company's assets, liabilities, and equity at a specific point in time. The balance sheet provides traders with insight into a company's financial strength and its ability to meet its obligations.

Cash Flow Statement: It provides information about a company's cash inflows and outflows over a specific period. It helps traders to evaluate a company's liquidity and its ability to generate cash to fund its operations.

By analyzing these financial statements, traders can make informed investment decisions. They can use financial ratios, such as the price-to-earnings ratio, to compare the financial performance of different companies and determine their relative value.

In summary, financial statements are essential for traders to evaluate a company's financial performance and position, make informed investment decisions, and manage risks effectively.

Income statement and different component of income statement :

An income statement is a financial statement that shows a company's revenues and expenses over a specific period. It helps to determine a company's profitability and financial performance.

The different components of an income statement include:

Revenue: This is the total amount of money a company earns from the sale of goods or services during a specific period.

Cost of Goods Sold (COGS): This represents the cost of producing or purchasing the goods or services that the company sells. It includes the cost of materials, labor, and other expenses directly related to production.

Gross Profit: This is the difference between revenue and the COGS. It represents the amount of money a company has left over after deducting the cost of goods sold.

Operating Expenses: These are the expenses incurred in running a business, such as salaries, rent, utilities, and advertising.

Operating Income: This is the profit a company earns from its operations after deducting operating expenses from gross profit.

Other Income/Expenses: These are non-operating items such as interest income or expense, gains or losses from the sale of assets, and taxes.

Net Income: This is the total profit or loss of a company for a given period. It is calculated by deducting all expenses, including taxes, from the company's revenue.

Earnings Per Share (EPS): This measures the amount of net income attributable to each share of common stock outstanding. It is calculated by dividing net income by the number of outstanding shares.

Dividends: These are payments made to shareholders from a company's profits.

An income statement helps investors and analysts assess a company's profitability, financial health, and future prospects. By analyzing the different components of an income statement, stakeholders can gain insights into the company's revenue streams, cost structure, and overall financial performance.

Balance sheet : A balance sheet is a financial statement that shows the company's financial position at a specific point in time. It provides a snapshot of the company's assets, liabilities, and equity, and it helps investors, creditors, and other stakeholders to assess the company's financial health.

Here's a breakdown of the components of a balance sheet:

Assets: This includes everything that the company owns or has a claim on. Examples of assets include cash, accounts receivable, inventory, property, plant and equipment, and investments.

Liabilities: This includes everything that the company owes to others. Examples of liabilities include accounts payable, loans, and accrued expenses.

Equity: This represents the residual interest in the assets of the company after deducting its liabilities. It includes things like the company's retained earnings, common stock, and preferred stock.

The balance sheet equation is Assets = Liabilities + Equity. This means that the total value of the assets must equal the total value of the liabilities and equity.

A balance sheet is an important tool for evaluating a company's financial position and can help investors make informed decisions about whether to invest in the company. It is typically included in a company's annual report and is also used by banks and other lenders when considering whether to extend credit to the company.

Key Notes :

- ***Check Net Sale and Net profit quaterly and Anualy***
- ***Mostly invest in those companies which are giving Dividend Regurlary***
- **Check cash flow of companies**
- **Check Debt of the Company**
- **Invest according Sector growth**

CHAPTER THREE

Stock Exchange

Stock Exchange :

A stock exchange is a marketplace where shares of publicly traded companies are bought and sold. In other words, it is a platform where investors can buy and sell ownership in companies. The exchange provides a transparent and regulated platform where buyers and sellers can interact and exchange shares at a fair price based on the supply and demand of the shares.

The stock exchange serves as a primary source of capital for companies looking to raise funds for growth and expansion. When a company decides to go public, it offers shares to the public through an initial public offering (IPO). Once the shares are listed on the stock exchange, investors can buy and sell them freely.

Stock exchanges play a crucial role in the global economy by providing a way for companies to raise capital, and by enabling investors to profit from the success of those companies. The most famous stock exchanges in the world include the National Stock Exchange of India (NSE), the NASDAQ, and the Tokyo Stock Exchange.

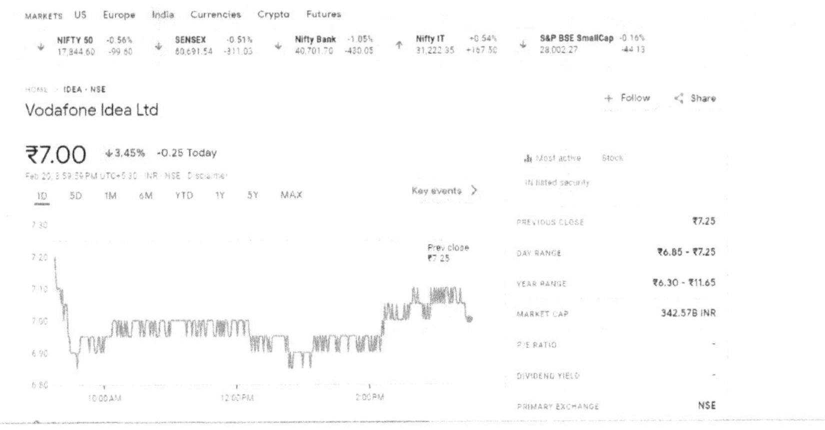

Chart

NSE & BSE :

NSE and BSE are the two major stock exchanges in India. NSE stands for National Stock Exchange and BSE stands for Bombay Stock Exchange.

The NSE was founded in 1992 and is headquartered in Mumbai. It is the largest stock exchange in India in terms of market capitalization and is known for its electronic trading platform. The NSE offers a wide range of financial products such as equities, futures and options, currency derivatives, and debt securities.

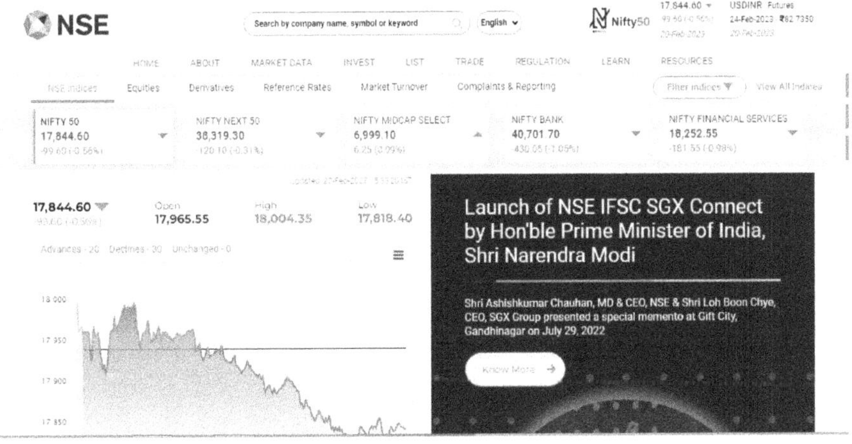

NSE

The BSE, on the other hand, is the oldest stock exchange in Asia, founded in 1875. It is headquartered in Mumbai as well and is known for its open outcry system of trading. The BSE also offers a range of financial products like equities, derivatives, mutual funds, and currency derivatives.

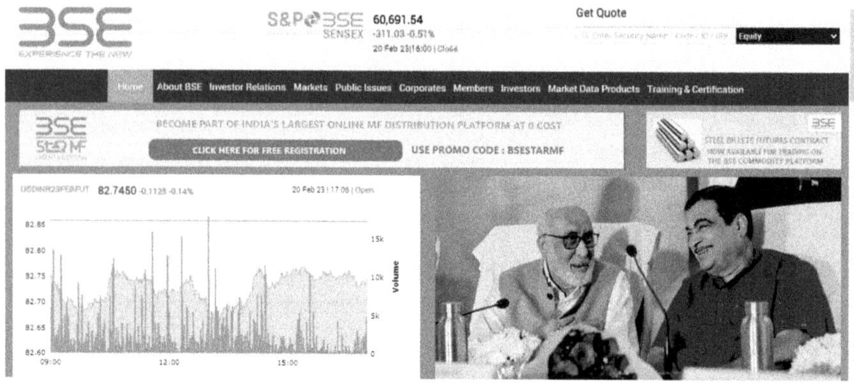

BSE

Both the NSE and BSE play a crucial role in the Indian economy, providing a platform for companies to raise capital and for investors to invest their money. They are regulated by the Securities and Exchange Board of India (SEBI) and operate under strict guidelines and regulations to ensure fair and transparent trading practices.

SEBI :

SEBI stands for Securities and Exchange Board of India. It is the regulatory body for the securities market in India. SEBI was established on April 12, 1992, under the Securities and Exchange Board of India Act, 1992.

SEBI's primary objective is to protect the interests of investors in securities and to promote the development and regulation of securities markets in India. Some of SEBI's key functions include regulating the stock exchanges, registering and regulating brokers and other intermediaries in the securities market, regulating the issuance and trading of securities, and investigating and taking enforcement action against market manipulation and insider trading.

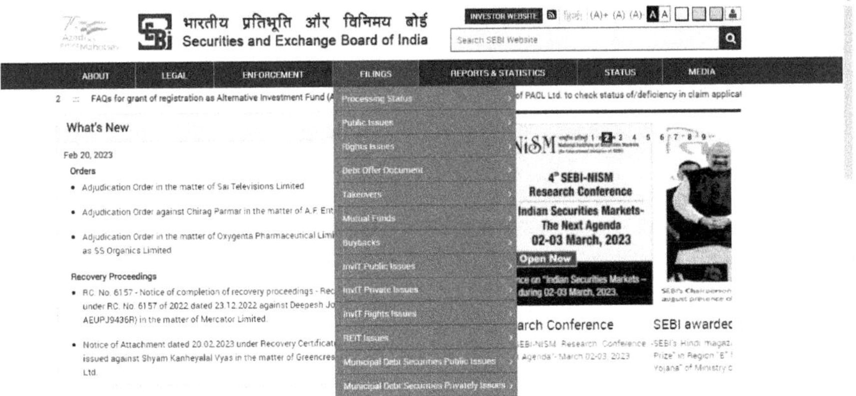

SEBI

SEBI plays a vital role in maintaining the integrity and stability of the Indian securities market, ensuring fair and transparent trading practices, and promoting investor education and awareness.

RBI :

RBI stands for Reserve Bank of India. It is the central bank of India and is responsible for regulating the country's monetary and financial system. The RBI was established on April 1, 1935, under the Reserve Bank of India Act, 1934.

The RBI performs various functions, including:

Issuing and managing the currency: The RBI is responsible for issuing and managing the currency in circulation in India.

Regulating the banking system: The RBI regulates and supervises the banking system in India to maintain financial stability.

Conducting monetary policy: The RBI formulates and implements monetary policy to control inflation and maintain price stability in the economy.

Managing foreign exchange reserves: The RBI manages the country's foreign exchange reserves and regulates foreign exchange transactions.

Developing the financial system: The RBI works towards developing the financial system in the country, including promoting financial inclusion and ensuring the safety and efficiency of payment systems.

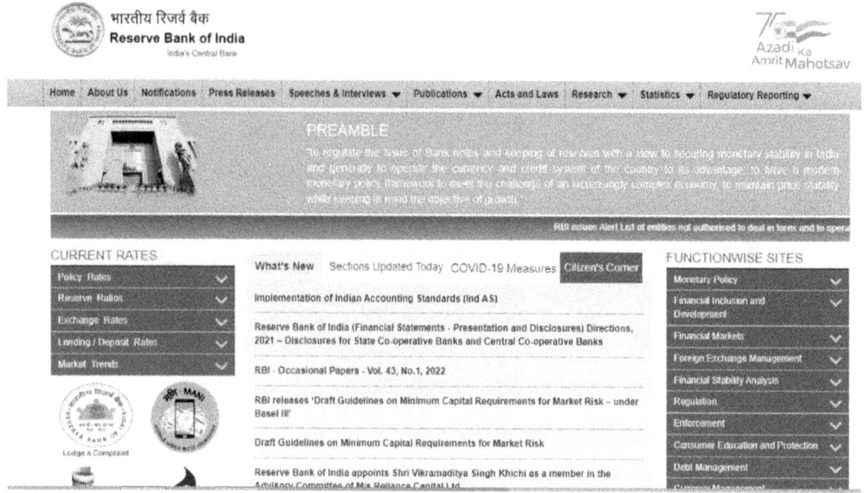

RBI

Overall, the RBI plays a crucial role in the Indian economy, and its policies and actions have a significant impact on the country's financial system and economic growth.

Primary Market & Secondary Market :

The primary market and the secondary market are two different segments of the financial market.

The primary market refers to the market where new securities, such as stocks or bonds, are first offered to the public through an initial public offering (IPO) or a private placement. In the primary market, companies or governments raise capital by issuing new securities and selling them to investors. The primary market is also referred to as the "new issue market."

The secondary market, on the other hand, is where securities that have already been issued in the primary market are bought and sold by investors. The secondary market is also referred to as the "stock market" or "stock exchange." The prices of securities in the secondary market are determined by market forces of supply and demand, and are influenced by factors such as company performance, economic conditions, and investor sentiment.

In summary, the primary market is where new securities are issued and sold for the first time, while the secondary market is where already issued securities are bought and sold by investors.

Sectors :

The Global Industry Classification Standard (GICS) is a widely used system for categorizing companies into sectors and sub-sectors. There are 11 main sectors in the GICS system:

1. **Energy**
2. **Materials**
3. **Industrials**
4. **Consumer Discretionary**
5. **Consumer Staples**
6. **Health Care**
7. **Financials**
8. **Information Technology**
9. **Communication Services**
10. **Utilities**
11. **Real Estate**

Each sector can be further divided into sub-sectors to provide more detailed categorization of companies. Investors often use sector analysis to evaluate the performance of a particular industry or to compare the performance of companies within the same sector. This can help investors make informed decisions about which stocks to buy or sell.

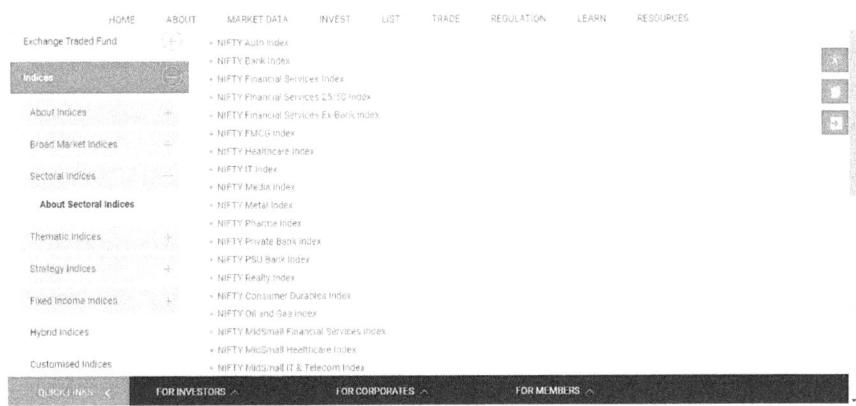

Nifty Sectors

Index :

The Nifty and BSE index are two major stock market indices in India.

The Nifty, officially known as the Nifty 50, is a stock market index of the National Stock Exchange of India (NSE), which is based in Mumbai. It consists of the 50 largest and most actively traded companies listed on the NSE. The Nifty 50 represents various sectors of the Indian economy such as finance, energy, information technology, and consumer goods. The Nifty 50 is considered one of the key benchmarks of the Indian stock market.

The BSE (Bombay Stock Exchange) index is also known as the Sensex, which is a stock market index of the Bombay Stock Exchange. It consists of the 30 largest and most actively traded companies listed on the BSE. The Sensex represents various sectors of the Indian economy such as finance, energy, consumer goods, and healthcare. The Sensex is considered one of the oldest and most widely followed stock market indices in India.

Market Watch - Indices

As on 20-Feb-2023 15:30:00 IST

Download (csv)

INDEX	CURRENT	%CHNG	OPEN	HIGH	LOW	PREV. CLOSE	PREV. DAY 16-FEB-2023	1W AGO 13-FEB-2023	1M AGO 20-JAN-2023	1Y AGO 18-FEB-2022	52W H	52W L	TODAY
BROAD MARKET INDICES													
NIFTY 50	17,844.60	-0.56	17,965.55	18,004.35	17,818.40	17,944.20	18,035.85	17,770.90	18,027.65	17,276.30	18,887.60	15,183.40	
NIFTY NEXT 50	38,319.30	-0.31	38,447.60	38,514.55	38,191.80	38,439.40	38,680.10	38,177.10	41,861.45	40,709.15	45,509.70	35,018.20	
NIFTY 100	17,626.90	-0.53	17,737.10	17,768.75	17,600.85	17,721.05	17,814.90	17,575.15	18,169.45	17,472.90	19,039.40	15,336.05	
NIFTY 200	9,233.55	-0.45	9,285.60	9,299.80	9,221.00	9,275.45	9,327.80	9,205.95	9,497.80	9,091.10	9,935.30	7,978.20	
NIFTY 500	14,938.65	-0.44	15,023.45	15,036.45	14,920.70	15,003.95	15,083.75	14,900.50	15,347.90	14,710.70	16,041.65	12,855.55	
NIFTY MIDCAP 50	8,647.30	-0.13	8,680.85	8,702.40	8,614.00	8,658.85	8,749.70	8,629.50	8,687.15	7,996.95	9,086.75	6,963.15	
NIFTY MIDCAP 100	30,666.90	0.08	30,715.00	30,826.40	30,491.60	30,642.05	30,886.50	30,565.35	31,099.80	28,934.35	32,939.30	25,048.15	
NIFTY SMALLCAP 100	9,385.20	-0.34	9,444.55	9,455.75	9,356.45	9,417.55	9,471.50	9,388.05	9,569.10	10,331.05	11,001.50	7,904.90	
INDIA VIX	13.39	2.27	13.09	13.71	10.92	13.09	12.59	13.68	13.79	22.17	33.97	10.17	
NIFTY MIDCAP 150	11,606.15	0.00	11,635.20	11,653.70	11,547.00	11,605.65	11,679.20	11,584.95	11,748.95	10,903.35	12,378.55	9,496.60	
NIFTY SMALLCAP 50	4,241.00	-0.48	4,272.90	4,277.05	4,228.30	4,261.40	4,294.85	4,256.55	4,288.65	4,755.60	5,076.35	3,588.30	
NIFTY SMALLCAP	9,133.15	-0.32	9,189.45	9,198.55	9,110.75	9,162.40	9,194.35	9,133.70	9,344.95	9,293.55	10,017.25	7,598.05	

Indices

Both the Nifty and BSE indices are used as benchmarks to measure the overall performance of the Indian stock market. Investors and traders use these indices as a tool to analyze the direction and trend of the stock market, and to make investment decisions based on their analysis.

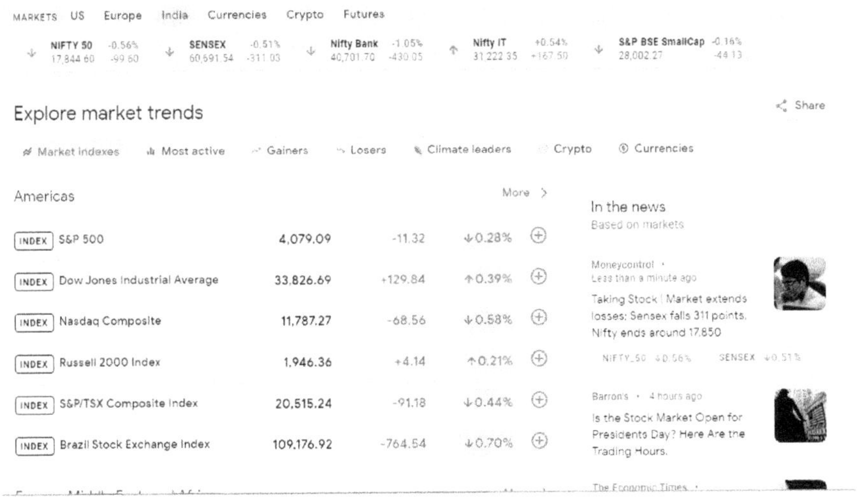

MARKETS US Europe India Currencies Crypto Futures

NIFTY 50	-0.56%	SENSEX	-0.51%	Nifty Bank	-1.05%	Nifty IT	+0.54%	S&P BSE SmallCap	-0.16%
17,844.60	-99.60	60,691.54	-311.03	40,701.70	-430.05	31,222.35	+167.50	28,002.27	-44.13

Explore market trends

Share

Market indexes Most active Gainers Losers Climate leaders Crypto Currencies

Americas

More >

INDEX S&P 500	4,079.09	-11.32	↓0.28%	⊕
INDEX Dow Jones Industrial Average	33,826.69	+129.84	↑0.39%	⊕
INDEX Nasdaq Composite	11,787.27	-68.56	↓0.58%	⊕
INDEX Russell 2000 Index	1,946.36	+4.14	↑0.21%	⊕
INDEX S&P/TSX Composite Index	20,515.24	-91.18	↓0.44%	⊕
INDEX Brazil Stock Exchange Index	109,176.92	-764.54	↓0.70%	⊕

In the news

Based on markets

Moneycontrol • Less than a minute ago

Taking Stock | Market extends losses: Sensex falls 311 points, Nifty ends around 17,850

NIFTY_50 ↓0.56% SENSEX ↓0.51%

Barron's • 4 hours ago

Is the Stock Market Open for Presidents Day? Here Are the Trading Hours.

The Economic Times •

world Markets

Sectors :

Nifty and BSE are two popular stock market indices in India. Both of these indices are used as benchmarks to measure the performance of the stock market as a whole. The Nifty index consists of the top 50 companies listed on the National Stock Exchange (NSE), while the BSE index consists of the top 30 companies listed on the Bombay Stock Exchange (BSE).

The companies listed in these indices belong to different sectors of the economy, such as healthcare, technology, financials, consumer goods, etc. Some of the popular sectors represented in the Nifty and BSE indices are:

Financial Services: This sector includes banks, insurance companies, asset management companies, and other financial service providers.

Information Technology: This sector includes companies that provide software development, IT consulting, hardware manufacturing, and other related services.

Consumer Goods: This sector includes companies that manufacture and sell products such as food and beverages, personal care products, and household items.

Healthcare: This sector includes companies that are involved in the manufacturing and distribution of pharmaceuticals, medical devices, and other healthcare products and services.

Energy: This sector includes companies that are involved in the exploration, production, and distribution of oil and gas, as well as companies that generate and distribute electricity.

Automobiles: This sector includes companies that manufacture and sell automobiles, two-wheelers, and other related products.

Infrastructure: This sector includes companies that are involved in the construction and maintenance of infrastructure such as roads, bridges, airports, and other related facilities.

Metals and Mining: This sector includes companies that are involved in the extraction, processing, and distribution of metals such as iron, steel, copper, and other related products.

These are just a few examples of the sectors represented in the Nifty and BSE indices. There are many other sectors and sub-sectors represented as well. The performance of these sectors and the companies within them can be influenced by a variety of factors, such as changes in government policies, global economic conditions, and shifts in consumer behavior, among others.

CDSL :

CDSL stands for Central Depository Services Limited, which is a leading depository in India. CDSL is a company that provides depository services for securities like stocks, bonds, and other financial instruments. It was established in 1997 and is headquartered in Mumbai, India.

CDSL provides services related to the holding, settlement, and transfer of securities in electronic form. It operates a central depository that allows investors to hold their securities in dematerialized form, which means that the physical certificates are converted into electronic form. This process is known as dematerialization.

CDSL provides its services to investors, brokers, and other financial institutions. Its services include dematerialization of securities, electronic settlement of trades, corporate actions, pledge and hypothecation of securities, and various other value-added services. CDSL is regulated by the Securities and Exchange Board of India (SEBI) and is a member of the International Securities Services Association (ISSA).

VIX:

VIX (CBOE Volatility Index) is a widely used financial metric that measures the expected volatility of the stock market over the next 30 days. It is often referred to as the "fear index" because it tends to rise during times of market uncertainty, instability, or panic.

The VIX is calculated based on the prices of options on the S&P 500 index. Options are financial instruments that give the holder the right, but not the obligation, to buy or sell an underlying asset (in this case, the S&P 500 index) at a specific price and time. The prices of these options reflect the market's expectation of future volatility in the S&P 500 index.

A higher VIX value indicates that the market is anticipating higher levels of volatility, while a lower VIX value indicates that the market is expecting lower levels of volatility. The VIX is often used by traders, investors, and analysts as a gauge of market sentiment and risk appetite, and can be used to hedge against market risk or speculate on volatility.

SECTORS IN THE STOCK MARKET

There are a lot of sectors that are present in the stock market, and in today's article, we are going to take a look at the Following are the main sectors of the Indian stock market-

Finance : It is the major sector in the stock market that includes commercial banks, insurance companies, non-banking financial companies, co-operatives, pension funds, mutual funds, and other smaller financial entities. India is having a diversified financial sector with strong growth of existing financial firms and new institutions entering into the business. As finance is the most important part of the economy, it is the most sensitive sector.

HDFC Bank, SBI, Bajaj Finance, Axis Bank, Muthoot Finance, etc. These are the major companies that belong to the finance sector.

•**Energy** : The energy sector is nothing but a group of companies that produce or supply energy. This sector mainly includes companies that perform the operation of exploration and development of oil or gas reserves, oil and gas drilling, and refining.

The revenue generated by this sector often fluctuates because it depends upon the price of natural gas, crude oil, and other commodities. Reliance Industries Limited, Power Grid Corporation of India, Oil & Natural Gas Corporation Ltd., NTPC Ltd., Bharat Petroleum Corp. Ltd., etc. These are the major companies present in Indian Stock Exchanges that belong to the energy sector.

•**Information Technology** : this sector mainly includes the companies which make software or companies that provide Internet-related services. IT sector is also one of the biggest sectors on the Indian Stock Exchange.

Companies in this sector provide various services such as manufacturing of electronics, creation of software, computers, or products and services relating to information technology. TCS, Infosys, Wipro, Tech Mahindra, HCL Tech, etc are the major companies of the IT sector.

• **Communication** : This sector includes companies that perform the operation of transmission of data through words, voice, audio, or video across the globe or the companies that offer telecom equipment or telecom-related services. This sector is an integral part of the Indian Economy as it simplifies and fastens the process of communication.

Bharti Airtel, Vodafone Idea LTD, Indus Towers LTD., etc. These are the major telecommunication companies.

•**Fast Moving Consumer Goods (FMCG) :**

This sector consists of a group of companies that produce packaged goods, i.e., goods that are produced, distributed, marketed, and consumed within a short period. FMCG sector is the 4th largest sector in the Indian Economy which comes under essential services.

Hindustan Unilever, Britannia Industries, Nestle, ITC, Dabur India, etc. These are the major companies that belong to the FMCG sector.

·**Automobile** : The automobile sector consists of companies involved in the development, design, manufacturing, and selling of motor vehicles. It is one of the biggest sectors in the Indian stock market by revenue. Maruti Suzuki, Tata Motors, Mahindra & Mahindra, Hero MotoCorp, etc. are the major companies of the automobile sector.

·**Pharmaceutical :**

The Pharma sector comprises companies involved in manufacturing medicines, vaccines, and other pharmaceutical drugs for use as medications. It is one of the most important sectors of the Indian economy because India is the largest provider of different vaccines used to prevent different diseases. India supplies over 50% of the global demands of various vaccines.

Sun Pharmaceutical, Divi's Laboratories, Cipla Ltd, Lupin, etc. are the major companies in the pharma sector.

·**Metal :**

The metal sector consists of companies involved in the extraction of metal and mineral reserves. Generally, metals are classified into two types; precious metals and industrial metals. Industrial metals are used in construction, manufacturing, and technology industries. Examples of industrial metals are zinc, iron, steel, aluminium, etc.

Precious metals are limited in supply and have a great value associated with them. Gold, silver, and platinum are examples of precious metals.

Tata Steel, JSW Steel, Hindustan Zinc, Hindalco are examples of major companies in the metal sector.

·**Infrastructure :**

The infra sector consists of companies involved in the development of power, bridges, dams, roads, and urban infrastructure development. This sector plays an important role when it comes to the overall development of the Indian Economy.

Larsen & Toubro Infrastructure Development Projects Limited, GMR Infrastructure Limited, Adani Port, and Special Economic Zone Limited are the major companies in the infrastructure sector.

·**Media** : The media sector consists of many different segments such as television, print, and films.Zee Entertainment Enterprises, Sun TV Network, PVR Ltd are the major companies in the media sector

Key Notes :

- **Deal with those Brokers which are registered with sebi**
- **Deal with those Brokers which has many Branches in the country dont trust on online site and websiteif they close then there will rise problem to recover your money.**
- **Deal with those brokers whose charges are less and which provide many services.**
- **Dont trust on Market it can change overnight**
- **always check taxes and charges of the govt and broker and trade according them.**

CHAPTER FOUR

Corporate Actions

Corporate Restructuring :

Corporate restructuring refers to the process of reorganizing a company's operations, structure, or ownership in order to improve its financial performance, efficiency, or strategic direction. This may involve making significant changes to a company's assets, liabilities, organizational structure, or business operations, including mergers, acquisitions, divestitures, spin-offs, joint ventures, and other forms of corporate restructuring.

Corporate restructuring is often undertaken in response to changing market conditions, new technologies, competitive pressures, or other external factors that impact a company's financial performance. It may also be initiated by internal factors, such as poor management, excessive debt, or ineffective business processes.

The primary objective of corporate restructuring is to create a more efficient and profitable company, with a better alignment of its resources and capabilities to its strategic goals. It can also help to reduce costs, increase revenue, improve cash flow, and create a more sustainable business model.

Corporate restructuring can be a complex and time-consuming process that requires careful planning, analysis, and execution. It may also involve significant legal and regulatory requirements, as well as employee and stakeholder communications. Companies often engage external consultants or advisors to help with the process of corporate restructuring.

Distributing Profit to Shareholder :

Distributing profits to shareholders is one of the key objectives of many companies. There are two main ways in which companies can distribute profits to their shareholders:

Dividends: A dividend is a portion of a company's profits that is paid out to its shareholders in proportion to the number of shares they own. Dividends are typically paid out on a regular basis, such as quarterly or annually. Companies may also pay out special dividends in addition to regular dividends if they have excess cash on hand.

Share buybacks: A share buyback, also known as a share repurchase, is when a company buys back its own shares from the market. This reduces the number of outstanding shares, which in turn increases the ownership stake of the remaining shareholders. Share buybacks can be used to return excess cash to shareholders, boost earnings per share, or support a company's share price.

The decision to distribute profits to shareholders is typically made by the company's board of directors, based on a variety of factors such as the company's financial performance, cash flow, growth prospects, and future capital needs. It is important for companies to strike a balance between distributing profits to shareholders and retaining earnings for future growth and investment opportunities.

Stock Split :

A stock split is a corporate action in which a company increases the number of outstanding shares by issuing additional shares to existing shareholders. The total value of the shares remains the same, but the number of shares outstanding increases, and the price per share decreases proportionally.

For example, in a 2-for-1 stock split, a shareholder who previously owned 100 shares would now own 200 shares, but the total value of their investment would remain the same.

Stock splits are usually undertaken by companies to make their shares more affordable to individual investors and increase liquidity in the market. Lower share prices can also make a company's shares more attractive to investors who may be deterred by higher prices. In addition, stock splits can increase trading activity and help to widen the company's shareholder base.

Stock splits are typically announced well in advance and are approved by the company's board of directors. They may be accompanied by other corporate actions, such as dividend increases or changes in the company's capital structure. Companies may also choose to undertake reverse stock splits, in which the number of outstanding shares is decreased and the price per share is increased, in order to raise the perceived value of their shares.

Right Issue :

A right issue, also known as a rights offering, is a type of corporate action in which a company offers its existing shareholders the opportunity to purchase additional shares of the company's stock, usually at a discounted price, in proportion to their existing holdings.

In a right issue, shareholders are given the option to exercise their rights by purchasing additional shares, or they can choose to sell their rights to someone else who may be interested in buying the new shares. The purpose of a right issue is usually to raise capital for the company, which can be used for various purposes such as funding expansion plans or paying down debt.

The price at which the new shares are offered to shareholders is typically lower than the current market price of the stock, which makes it an attractive opportunity for existing shareholders to increase their ownership in the company. However, if a shareholder chooses not to exercise their rights or sell them, their ownership stake in the company will be diluted as a result of the new shares being issued.

Right issues are typically announced by companies through a press release or other public announcement, and shareholders are given a certain period of time to exercise their rights or sell them to someone else. The terms and conditions of the right issue, including the number of shares being offered and the subscription price, are outlined in a prospectus that is made available to shareholders.

Merger & Acquisition :

Merger and acquisition (M&A) refer to the consolidation of two or more companies into a single entity. The terms are often used interchangeably, but they have slightly different meanings.

Mergers occur when two companies of roughly equal size agree to join forces and become a single entity. In this case, both companies' stocks are surrendered, and new stock is issued for the combined entity. Mergers can be classified into different types, including horizontal, vertical, and conglomerate mergers.

Acquisitions, on the other hand, occur when one company purchases another company. The company that is being acquired is typically smaller than the acquiring company. Acquisitions can be friendly or hostile, depending on whether the target company agrees to be acquired or not.

M&A activities are usually driven by the desire to achieve economies of scale, increase market share, expand into new markets, or diversify the company's products or services. M&A can be a complex and lengthy process that involves legal, financial, and strategic considerations. It can also have significant impacts on employees, customers, and shareholders of both companies.

Demerger :

A demerger, also known as a spin-off, is a corporate restructuring strategy in which a company separates out one or more of its business units or subsidiaries into a standalone entity. The new entity may be sold, listed on the stock exchange, or distributed among the shareholders of the original company.

A demerger can be carried out for a variety of reasons. For example, it may be done to enable the separated business unit to pursue its own strategic goals, or to unlock shareholder value by allowing investors to focus on specific businesses or markets. A demerger may also be undertaken to simplify the structure of a complex conglomerate or to facilitate a merger or acquisition.

There are various ways to carry out a demerger. For example, a company may create a new subsidiary and transfer ownership of the business unit to that subsidiary. The subsidiary may then be listed on the stock exchange or sold to a third party. Alternatively, the company may distribute shares in the subsidiary to its existing shareholders in proportion to their holdings. In some cases, a demerger may involve the transfer of assets and liabilities from the original company to the new entity.

Demergers can have significant financial and operational implications for both the original company and the newly created entity. As such, they are typically subject to careful planning and consideration, including analysis of the tax, accounting, legal, and regulatory implications of the demerger.

Bonus Issue :

A bonus issue, also known as a scrip issue or a capitalization issue, is an issuance of additional shares to existing shareholders by a company at no additional cost. This means that the shareholders do not have to pay for the newly issued shares, and they receive them in proportion to their existing holdings.

The purpose of a bonus issue is to increase the number of shares outstanding without diluting the ownership of the existing shareholders. By increasing the number of shares outstanding, the value of each share is reduced, but the overall value of the company remains the same.

Bonus issues are often used by companies as a way to reward their existing shareholders and increase the liquidity of their stock. They are also used as a way to reduce the price per share, making the stock more affordable for retail investors.

Bonus issues are accounted for by transferring funds from the company's reserves to its share capital account. This means that the company's reserves are reduced, but its share capital increases. As a result, the company's balance sheet remains unchanged, but the number of shares outstanding increases.

IPO :

IPO stands for Initial Public Offering. It refers to the process of a private company going public by selling its shares of stock to the public for the first time.

In an IPO, the company typically works with an investment bank or underwriter to determine the offering price, the number of shares to be sold, and the timing of the offering. The underwriter also helps the company navigate the regulatory requirements of going public, such as filing a registration statement with the Securities and Exchange of India

Once the IPO is completed, the company's shares will be listed on a stock exchange, such as the National Stock Exchange or BSE, where they can be bought and sold by investors. The funds raised from the IPO can be used by the company for various purposes, such as expanding the business, paying off debt, or investing in research and development.

Dividend :

A dividend is a payment made by a corporation to its shareholders, usually in the form of cash or additional shares of stock. Dividends are a portion of the company's profits that are distributed to its shareholders, and they are typically paid out on a regular basis, such as quarterly or annually.

The amount of the dividend paid to each shareholder is determined by the company's board of directors and is based on various factors, such as the company's financial performance, its cash reserves, and its growth plans. Some companies may also offer special one-time dividends in addition to their regular dividends.

Dividends can be an important source of income for investors, particularly those who rely on their investments to generate regular cash flow. However, not all companies pay dividends, and some may choose to reinvest their profits back into the business instead. Additionally, the value of a company's stock can be affected by its dividend policy, with investors often valuing stocks that pay consistent and growing dividends more highly.

Board of directors and promoters :

The board of directors and promoters are two important groups of individuals involved in the management and decision-making of a company.

The board of directors is a group of individuals elected by the shareholders of a company to oversee the management of the company and make decisions on behalf of the shareholders. The board typically consists of both executive and non-executive directors, with the former being responsible for the day-to-day management of the company and the latter providing independent oversight and guidance. The board of directors is responsible for setting the strategic direction of the company, making major decisions on issues such as mergers and acquisitions, and appointing and supervising the executive management team.

Promoters, on the other hand, are individuals or groups who start a company and take on the initial financial risk. They are usually the ones who come up with the idea for the business, invest their own money to get it off the ground, and work to build its reputation and customer base. Promoters may also be involved in the day-to-day management of the company, although this is not always the case.

While the board of directors and promoters have different roles in a company, they both play important roles in its success. The board provides oversight and guidance to ensure that the company is being run in the best interests of its shareholders, while the promoters are responsible for the initial vision and growth of the company. Together, they work to ensure the long-term success of the business.

Debentures

Debentures are a type of long-term debt security issued by companies or government entities to raise funds. Debentures are essentially IOUs that promise to pay back the principal amount plus interest at a specified future date. They are generally unsecured, meaning that they are not backed by any collateral, and are therefore riskier than secured debt.

Debentures are usually issued to raise funds for long-term projects, such as the construction of a new facility or the acquisition of another company. They are typically sold to institutional investors, such as pension funds, insurance companies, and mutual funds, as well as to individual investors.

Debentures come in different varieties, including convertible debentures, which can be converted into equity shares of the issuing company at a predetermined price, and non-convertible debentures, which cannot be converted into equity shares. They may also be issued with different interest rates, maturity dates, and redemption provisions.

Investors in debentures are primarily interested in receiving a steady stream of interest payments and the eventual return of their principal investment. However, as with all investments, there is a risk that the issuer may default on its obligations, resulting in a loss for the investor. As a result, it is important to carefully evaluate the creditworthiness of the issuer before investing in debentures.

Key Notes :

- **Divide your capital into 10 equal risk parts**
- **Never overtrade**
- **Never place order for Buy/sell without stop loss condition**
- **Never let profit turn into loss**
- **Trade with the trend**

CHAPTER FIVE

Financial Statement

A financial statement is a report that summarizes an organization's financial activities and position over a specific period, typically a fiscal year. Financial statements provide insight into an organization's overall financial health by presenting a detailed breakdown of its revenues, expenses, assets, and liabilities.

There are three primary financial statements that companies produce, which are:

Income statement (or profit and loss statement): This statement shows the company's revenues and expenses over a specific period, typically a year. It indicates whether the company has made a profit or incurred a loss during that period.

Balance sheet: This statement presents the company's assets, liabilities, and equity at a specific point in time, typically at the end of the fiscal year. It provides a snapshot of the company's financial position and indicates how much it owns and owes.

Cash flow statement: This statement presents the company's cash inflows and outflows over a specific period, typically a year. It shows where the company's cash is coming from and how it is being spent.

Overall, financial statements are essential for businesses, investors, creditors, and other stakeholders, as they provide a clear understanding of an organization's financial health and help inform decision-making.

How financial statement helps in trading :

Financial statements, such as the balance sheet, income statement, and cash flow statement, provide valuable information that can help traders make more informed trading decisions. Here are some ways financial statements can help in trading:

Assessing a company's financial health: Financial statements allow traders to evaluate a company's profitability, liquidity, and solvency. This information can help traders determine whether a company is financially stable and has the potential to generate returns.

Identifying trends and patterns: Traders can use financial statements to identify trends and patterns in a company's financial performance over time. This can help traders anticipate future changes in a company's stock price and adjust their trading strategies accordingly.

Analyzing valuation metrics: Financial statements provide data on a company's market capitalization, earnings per share, and other valuation metrics. Traders can use this information to assess whether a company's stock is undervalued or overvalued and make trading decisions based on their analysis.

Comparing companies: Financial statements allow traders to compare the financial performance of different companies in the same industry. This can help traders identify companies that are performing well relative to their peers and make trades based on their comparative analysis.

Overall, financial statements provide traders with valuable information that can help them make more informed trading decisions. However, it's important to note that financial statements are just one of many factors that should be considered when making trading decisions, and traders should always conduct thorough research and analysis before making any trades.

Margin :

Margin in trading refers to the amount of money or collateral that a trader must deposit with their broker in order to open and maintain a position in a financial market. Margin allows traders to control a larger position in the market than they would be able to if they only used their own capital.

The amount of margin required by the broker typically depends on several factors, including the size of the position, the volatility of the market, and the trader's level of experience. Margin can be calculated as a percentage of the total position value, known as the margin requirement.

When a trader opens a position using margin, they are essentially borrowing money from the broker. As such, they are subject to interest charges on the borrowed amount. In addition, if the market moves against the trader and the position incurs losses, the broker may issue a margin call, requiring the trader to deposit additional funds to cover the losses and maintain the position.

Margin trading can be a powerful tool for experienced traders to leverage their capital and potentially generate higher returns, but it also carries significant risks, and should be approached with caution.

Line Chart

Overview F&O Events News

Performance

Today's Low	Today's High
111.30	113.10

52W Low	52W High
82.70	138.67

Open Price	Prev. Close	Volume	Value
111.55	112.00	3,41,07,244	383 Cr

Stock live Data

Open Price : Open price refers to the price at which a financial asset, such as a stock, begins trading at the start of a trading day. It is the first price at which the asset is sold after the opening bell. The open price can be higher or lower than the previous day's closing price, depending on various factors such as market conditions, news events, and investor sentiment.

Previous Close : Previous close, on the other hand, refers to the price at which the financial asset ended trading on the previous trading day. It is the last price at which the asset was sold before the market closed. The previous close can be used as a reference point for evaluating the performance of the asset in the current trading day, as it provides a baseline for comparison. If the current price is higher than the previous close, it indicates that the asset is performing well, and vice versa.

Volume :

In trading, volume refers to the total number of shares or contracts traded in a particular security or market during a specific time period. Volume is a crucial indicator of market activity, as it helps traders and investors gauge the strength and liquidity of a market.

High trading volume typically indicates that there is a lot of buying and selling activity in the market, which can create opportunities for profitable trades. On the other hand, low trading volume can suggest that the market is quiet, with fewer participants buying and selling, which can make it more difficult to find good trading opportunities.

In addition to its use as a market indicator, volume is also important for technical analysis. For example, traders often use volume indicators such as on-balance volume (OBV) or volume-weighted average price (VWAP) to help identify trends and support or resistance levels in a market.

Value :

Value in trading refers to the perceived worth of an asset or financial instrument that is being bought or sold in the financial markets. The value of an asset is determined by various factors, including its supply and demand, market sentiment, economic conditions, and company performance.

Traders seek to identify assets that are undervalued or overvalued based on their analysis of these factors, and then make trading decisions accordingly. For example, if a trader believes that a particular stock is undervalued, they may buy it in the hope that its value will increase in the future. Conversely, if they believe that a stock is overvalued, they may sell it in the hope of profiting from a subsequent price decline.

Ultimately, the value of an asset is subjective and can vary depending on the individual trader's perspective and analysis. Successful traders are those who can accurately assess the value of an asset and make profitable trades based on that assessment.

Today High & Low :

In trading, the terms "high" and "low" refer to the highest and lowest prices reached by a particular financial asset during a trading day. The high price is the highest price at which a particular asset was traded during the day, while the low price is the lowest price at which the asset was traded.

For example, if the high price of a stock for the day was $50 and the low price was $40, it means that during the trading day, the stock traded at prices ranging from $40 to $50. Traders and investors pay close attention to the high and low prices of assets because they provide important information about the price range in which the asset is trading, and can be used to inform trading decisions.

52 week High & Low :

The 52-week high and low refer to the highest and lowest prices that a stock has traded at over the past year, typically measured from the current date. These values can be useful indicators of a stock's recent performance and volatility.

For example, if a stock is currently trading close to its 52-week high, it may be seen as a positive signal of strong performance and investor confidence. Conversely, if a stock is trading close to its 52-week low, it may indicate that investors are uncertain about the company's prospects.

Investors often use the 52-week range to help determine whether a stock is overvalued or undervalued. If a stock is trading near its 52-week high and has a high price-to-earnings ratio, for instance, it may be considered overvalued. On the other hand, a stock trading near its 52-week low with a low P/E ratio may be considered undervalued.

It's important to note that the 52-week high and low values are not the only factors to consider when making investment decisions. It's also important to look at the company's financials, management, industry trends, and other relevant information.

Fundamentals

Market Cap	₹1,35,894Cr	ROE	42.56%
P/E Ratio(TTM)	4.77	EPS(TTM)	23.49
P/B Ratio	1.20	Dividend Yield	4.55%
Industry P/E	12.00	Book Value	88.03
Debt to Equity	0.81	Face Value	1

Understand Fundamentals

Fundamentals

Market Capital :

Market capitalization (market cap) is a measure of the total value of a company's outstanding shares of stock in the stock market. It is calculated by multiplying the total number of outstanding shares of stock by the current market price of one share.

In trading, market capitalization is an important metric that is used to evaluate the size and performance of publicly traded companies. Companies with larger market capitalizations are generally considered to be more stable and less risky than companies with smaller market capitalizations.

Investors and traders often use market capitalization as a factor when making investment decisions. For example, some investors prefer to invest in large-cap companies because they tend to have a more established track record, higher liquidity, and lower volatility than smaller companies.

On the other hand, some investors may prefer to invest in small-cap or mid-cap companies because they may have greater growth potential and can offer higher returns if successful. However, smaller companies can also be riskier and more volatile, and their stocks may be less liquid and harder to trade.

Overall, market capitalization is an important metric in trading that can help investors and traders evaluate the size and performance of companies and make informed investment decisions based on their risk tolerance and investment goals.

P/E Ratio & PB Ratio :

PE ratio (Price-to-Earnings Ratio) and PB ratio (Price-to-Book Ratio) are two commonly used financial metrics to evaluate the relative value of a company's stock.

PE ratio is the ratio of the company's stock price to its earnings per share (EPS). It indicates how much investors are willing to pay for each dollar of the company's earnings. A higher PE ratio generally suggests that investors are optimistic about the company's future growth prospects, whereas a lower PE ratio indicates that the company's earnings are relatively low or uncertain.

PB ratio, on the other hand, is the ratio of the company's stock price to its book value per share (BVPS). BVPS is the company's net assets (assets minus liabilities) divided by the number of outstanding shares. PB ratio indicates how much investors are willing to pay for each dollar of the company's net assets. A higher PB ratio suggests that investors are willing to pay a premium for the company's net assets, which can be an indication of the company's growth potential and/or the quality of its assets.

Industry P/B Ratio :

The industry P/B ratio varies depending on the sector and the current market conditions. As of my knowledge cutoff in September 2021, the average P/B ratio for the S&P 500 index, which represents a broad range of industries, was around 4.3. However, this can change based on market fluctuations and other factors that affect a company's financial performance. It is important to note that the P/B ratio should not be used in isolation and should be considered alongside other financial metrics and factors when making investment decisions.

Debt to Equity :

Debt to Equity is a financial ratio that compares a company's total debt to its total equity. It is used to determine the extent to which a company is financing its operations with debt versus equity.

The formula for calculating the debt to equity ratio is as follows:

Debt to Equity Ratio = Total Debt / Total Equity

Total debt refers to all the liabilities that a company has, including both short-term and long-term debt. Total equity refers to the total value of the company's assets minus its liabilities.

A high debt to equity ratio indicates that a company is heavily reliant on debt financing, which can increase its financial risk. On the other hand, a low debt to equity ratio indicates that a company is relying more on equity financing, which can be less risky but may limit its ability to take advantage of growth opportunities.

The ideal debt to equity ratio varies depending on the industry and the company's specific circumstances. In general, a ratio of 1 or lower is considered to be healthy, while a ratio above 2 may indicate financial distress. However, it is important to interpret the ratio in the context of other financial metrics and the company's overall financial health.

ROE :

ROE stands for Return on Equity, which is a financial ratio that measures the profitability of a company in relation to the amount of equity invested by shareholders.

ROE is calculated by dividing the net income of a company by its average shareholders' equity during a specific period of time. The result is expressed as a percentage and indicates how much profit a company generates for each dollar of equity invested by its shareholders.

A high ROE indicates that a company is effectively using the funds invested by shareholders to generate profits, while a low ROE suggests that the company is not efficiently using its equity to generate returns.

ROE is an important metric for investors and analysts to evaluate the performance of a company and compare it with its peers. However, it should be used in conjunction with other financial ratios and metrics to gain a comprehensive understanding of a company's financial health and performance.

EPS :

Earnings per share (EPS) is a financial ratio that measures the amount of profit a company has earned for each outstanding share of its common stock. It is calculated by dividing a company's net income by the number of outstanding shares of its common stock.

The formula for calculating earnings per share is:

EPS = (Net Income - Preferred Dividends) / Average Outstanding Shares

Where:

Net Income is the company's total income after deducting all expenses.

Preferred Dividends is the amount of money paid to preferred stockholders, if any.

Average Outstanding Shares is the average number of shares outstanding during the period.

Earnings per share is an important metric used by investors to evaluate a company's financial performance and profitability. A higher EPS indicates that a company is generating more profit per share, which is generally considered a positive sign for investors.

Dividend Yield :

Dividend yield is a financial ratio that represents the percentage of a company's annual dividend payment in relation to its stock price. It is calculated by dividing the annual dividend per share by the current stock price, then multiplying by 100 to express the result as a percentage.

The formula for dividend yield is:

Dividend Yield = (Annual Dividend per Share / Stock Price) x 100

For example, if a company pays an annual dividend of $1 per share and its stock is currently trading at $50 per share, the dividend yield would be:

Dividend Yield = (1 / 50) x 100 = 2%

This means that the company is paying out 2% of its stock price in dividends each year. Dividend yield is a measure of how much income an investor can expect to receive from their investment in the form of dividends. It is often used by investors as a way to evaluate the relative attractiveness of different dividend-paying stocks.

Book Value :

Book value is a financial term that refers to the net value of a company's assets, as recorded in its accounting books. It is calculated by subtracting the total liabilities of a company from the total assets, and it represents the amount of equity in the company that would be left over if all of its assets were sold and all of its debts were paid off.

Book value is an important metric for investors and analysts, as it can provide a sense of the underlying value of a company's assets. However, it is important to note that book value does not necessarily reflect the market value of a company's assets, which can be influenced by a wide range of factors, such as supply and demand, market sentiment, and economic conditions.

In addition, the book value of a company's assets may not reflect their true market value if they are significantly depreciated, or if they are carried on the books at a historical cost that does not reflect their current market value. For these reasons, investors often use a range of different metrics and approaches to analyze the value and performance of companies.

Face value :

Face value generally refers to the value or worth of something as stated on its surface or official documentation, without taking into account any additional factors such as market value, condition, or other circumstances that may affect its true worth.

In finance, face value usually refers to the nominal value of a financial instrument such as a bond, note, or stock, which is the amount that is printed on the instrument and represents the principal amount that will be repaid upon maturity. This is distinct from the market value of the instrument, which may be higher or lower than its face value based on various market factors such as supply and demand, interest rates, or economic conditions.

In the context of coins and currency, face value is the denomination of the coin or bill, and represents the amount of money that it is worth in legal tender. However, the actual value of a coin or bill may be worth more than its face value due to its rarity, condition, or historical significance.

Overall, face value is an important concept in various fields, and it is crucial to distinguish it from other types of value that may affect its true worth.

CAGR :

CAGR stands for Compound Annual Growth Rate. It is a measure of the annual growth rate of an investment over a period of time, assuming that the investment has been compounding at a steady rate.

The CAGR is calculated by taking the ending value of the investment, dividing it by the beginning value, raising that result to the power of 1/n (where n is the number of years in the investment period), and then subtracting 1.

For example, if an investment had an initial value of $10,000 and a final value of $15,000 after five years, the CAGR would be:

CAGR = (15000/10000)^(1/5) - 1 = 8.14%

This means that the investment grew at an average annual rate of 8.14% over the five-year period. The CAGR is useful for comparing the performance of investments with different time periods and can help investors understand the annualized return on their investments.

Fundamentals of stock :

Stocks represent ownership in a company. When you buy a stock, you are buying a small part of the company and become a shareholder. The value of the stock can increase or decrease based on the performance of the company, market conditions, and other factors.

Here are some fundamental concepts of stock investing:

Price: The price of a stock is determined by the supply and demand of buyers and sellers in the market. The stock price is usually quoted in dollars per share.

Market Capitalization: Market capitalization (or market cap) is the total value of all outstanding shares of a company's stock. It is calculated by multiplying the number of shares by the current market price per share.

Dividends: Some companies pay a portion of their profits to shareholders in the form of dividends. Dividends can provide investors with a regular income stream, but not all companies pay dividends.

Earnings Per Share (EPS): EPS is a measure of a company's profitability. It is calculated by dividing the company's net income by the number of outstanding shares. A higher EPS indicates a more profitable company.

Price-to-Earnings (P/E) Ratio: The P/E ratio is a valuation ratio that compares a company's stock price to its earnings per share. A higher P/E ratio indicates that investors are willing to pay more for each dollar of earnings.

Stock Splits: A stock split occurs when a company increases the number of outstanding shares, but the total value of the shares remains the same. For example, in a 2-for-1 stock split, each shareholder receives two shares for every one share they previously owned.

Stock Buybacks: A stock buyback occurs when a company purchases its own shares in the open market. This can increase the value of the remaining shares by reducing the number of outstanding shares.

It's important to do your research and understand the fundamentals of the companies you invest in before buying their stock. This can help you make informed investment decisions and reduce the risk of losing money.

VAR :

Value at Risk (VaR) is a statistical measure that aims to quantify the potential loss that an investment portfolio, business, or financial instrument may experience over a specific time period, at a certain level of confidence.

VaR estimates the maximum loss that a portfolio could experience, with a certain probability, over a defined period of time. For instance, a company might use VaR to estimate the potential loss of its investment portfolio over the next week, assuming a 95% confidence level. This means that the company believes that the portfolio will lose more than the VaR estimate only 5% of the time.

VaR can be calculated using various statistical models, such as Monte Carlo simulation, historical simulation, or parametric models. The choice of model will depend on the characteristics of the portfolio, the available data, and the desired level of accuracy.

VaR is widely used in the financial industry to measure and manage risks, to determine capital requirements, and to set limits on trading activities. However, it is important to note that VaR is not a perfect measure of risk and has limitations, as it is based on historical data and assumptions about future market behavior, which can be volatile and unpredictable.

Value at Risk (VaR) is a statistical measure used to estimate the potential loss of an investment or portfolio of investments over a specific time period with a given level of confidence. VaR Margin is the additional margin required by a clearinghouse or exchange to cover potential losses beyond the daily price limit for a particular market.

VaR margin is calculated by applying a pre-determined confidence level to the VaR calculation. For example, if the VaR for a portfolio is estimated to be $10,000 with a 99% confidence level, the VaR margin would be the additional amount required to cover potential losses beyond $10,000 with 99% confidence.

VaR margin is used by clearinghouses and exchanges to reduce the risk of default by market participants. By requiring traders to post additional margin, the clearinghouse or exchange can ensure that losses beyond the daily price limit are covered, reducing the risk of a default that could affect the entire market.

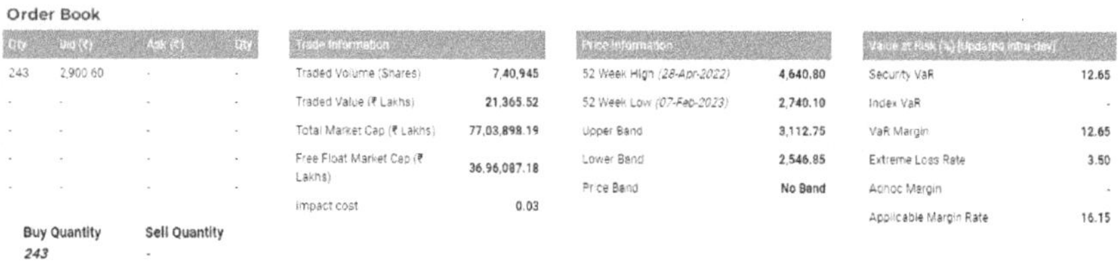

Order Book

Qty	Bid (₹)	Ask (₹)	Qty
243	2,900.60	-	-
-	-	-	-
-	-	-	-
-	-	-	-
-	-	-	-

Buy Quantity	Sell Quantity
243	-

Trade Information	
Traded Volume (Shares)	7,40,945
Traded Value (₹ Lakhs)	21,365.52
Total Market Cap (₹ Lakhs)	77,03,898.19
Free Float Market Cap (₹ Lakhs)	36,96,087.18
Impact cost	0.03

Price Information	
52 Week High *(28-Apr-2022)*	4,640.80
52 Week Low *(07-Feb-2023)*	2,740.10
Upper Band	3,112.75
Lower Band	2,546.85
Price Band	No Band

Value at Risk (%) (Updated intra-day)	
Security VaR	12.65
Index VaR	-
VaR Margin	12.65
Extreme Loss Rate	3.50
Adhoc Margin	-
Applicable Margin Rate	16.15

VAR

"**Pledging** : in stock" usually refers to the practice of using stock as collateral for a loan. In this process, a borrower pledges their stock holdings as collateral for a loan from a lender. The lender will hold the stock as security and lend the borrower an amount of money that is typically a percentage of the value of the stock.

The borrower retains ownership of the stock, but the lender has the right to sell the stock to recover the loan amount if the borrower defaults on the loan. The amount of the loan and the interest rate charged will depend on factors such as the value of the stock, the creditworthiness of the borrower, and market conditions.

Pledging stock can be a useful way for individuals or companies to raise capital quickly, without having to sell their stock holdings outright. However, it carries risks, as if the stock value drops significantly, the borrower may be required to provide additional collateral or repay the loan to avoid having their stock sold by the lender.

Key Notes :

- **Analyse all information and compare with other companies or sectors.**
- **Booking profit is more important rather than looking profit**
- **Dont trade if trend not clear**
- **Dont follow tips only ,research only trade when things are show on chart rather than mind.**
- **use right orders only which are cheap and best at right timing.**

CHAPTER SIX

Mutual Fund

A mutual fund is a type of investment vehicle that pools money from multiple investors to purchase a diversified portfolio of stocks, bonds, or other securities. The fund is managed by professional fund managers who invest the pooled money in various asset classes with the aim of generating a return for the investors.

When an investor buys shares in a mutual fund, they are effectively buying a portion of the fund's overall portfolio. The price of the shares is determined by the net asset value (NAV) of the fund, which is calculated by dividing the total value of the fund's assets by the number of shares outstanding.

The fund's returns are based on the performance of the underlying investments. Any income generated from dividends or interest on the securities is usually distributed to the fund's investors in the form of dividends. Additionally, the value of the mutual fund shares can appreciate or depreciate based on the performance of the underlying investments.

Mutual funds offer several benefits to investors, including diversification, professional management, liquidity, and accessibility. However, it's important to note that mutual funds are subject to market risk, and the value of the investments can fluctuate. Investors should carefully consider their investment goals, risk tolerance, and the fees associated with the mutual fund before investing.

Different types of fund

Fund Manager :

A fund manager in a mutual fund is a person or a team of people responsible for making investment decisions on behalf of the mutual fund's investors. The fund manager's primary goal is to generate returns for the fund's investors by investing in a diversified portfolio of stocks, bonds, or other securities.

The fund manager is responsible for analyzing the financial markets, researching potential investments, and making decisions about which securities to buy, hold, or sell in the fund's portfolio. The fund manager is also responsible for monitoring the performance of the fund and making adjustments to the portfolio as necessary to ensure that the fund's investment objectives are being met.

Fund managers are typically highly experienced and have a deep understanding of the financial markets and the securities in which they invest. They are also subject to rigorous regulation and oversight by government agencies and industry organizations to ensure that they act in the best interests of their investors.

Mutual Fund category :

Mutual funds can be categorized in a number of ways, but here are some common mutual fund categories:

Equity Funds: These funds invest primarily in stocks, which can be of various types such as large-cap, mid-cap, small-cap, or sector-specific stocks.

Debt Funds: These funds invest in fixed-income securities such as government bonds, corporate bonds, or other debt instruments.

Balanced Funds: These funds invest in a mix of equity and debt securities to provide a balanced portfolio for investors.

Money Market Funds: These funds invest in short-term, low-risk debt securities such as treasury bills, certificates of deposit, and commercial paper.

Index Funds: These funds track a specific market index, such as the Nifty 50 or the BSE, and aim to replicate the performance of the index.

Specialty Funds: These funds invest in specific sectors or themes such as real estate, energy, or socially responsible investments.

Fund of Funds: These funds invest in other mutual funds, providing investors with diversification across a range of asset classes and investment strategies.

Global or International Funds: These funds invest in companies and securities outside of the investor's home country, providing exposure to global markets.

Debt Mutual Funds primarily invest in fixed-income instruments like Government securities, corporate bonds, and other debt instruments. They are not affected by stock market volatility and hence, can offer more stable returns compared to equity mutual funds. The types of debt mutual funds are differentiated on the basis of the maturity period of the securities they hold. Let's look at a few types of debt mutual funds-

Liquid Funds : invest in debt securities and higher-rated securities which have a maturity period of fewer than 91 days. This makes them relatively less risky than most other categories because a lower maturity mitigates any interest rate volatility (which is the risk of loss resulting from a change in interest rates). Liquid funds are a good avenue for parking emergency funds alternative to bank savings accounts.

Overnight Funds : invest in securities with a maturity of one day. These funds come with low risks safety again because of shorter maturity periods, the interest rate risk is on the lower side. These are commonly used by corporates to park their funds.

Money Market Funds : invest mainly in government securities (known as treasury bills) and similar instruments, which are short-term with maturity periods less than one year. These funds are suitable for investors looking for stable and non-volatile funds as interest risk is less.

Banking & PSU Funds : invest at least 80% of their investment in debt securities of banks, public sector undertakings, municipal bonds, public financial institutions etc. They can be better suited for investors looking for short to medium-term investment tenure.

Ways/modes of Mutual Fund Investment :

An investor can invest in mutual funds in the following ways:

Lumpsum – When you want to invest a significant amount in a mutual fund at one go. For example, if you had a sum of Rs 1 lakh to invest then you could go in for lumpsum investment and invest the entire amount of Rs 1.0 lakh at one go in a mutual fund of your choice. The units allotted to you will depend on the NAV of that fund on that particular day. If the NAV is Rs 1000, you will end up getting 100 units of the mutual fund.

SIP – You also have an option to invest small amounts periodically. In the above example, say, you don't have Rs 1 Lakh but can commit to an investment of Rs 10,000 per month for 10 months, you can align your investments with your cash flows. This way of investing is known as Systematic Investment Plan (SIP). SIP encourages regular investment of fixed amounts bi-monthly, monthly, quarterly and so on, depending on your need and the options available with the mutual fund.

Key notes :

- **Withdraw Portion of profit slowly slowly so you can always be in the profit and can use that money.**
- **Dont hurry about closing your stock and dont late to exit before high loss.**
- **Never buy a stock to get only dividend also buy for return on your investment**
- **Never averages your losses.**
- **Take big profit and small loss**
- **Dont take big risk which you cant afford that loss save your capital**

CHAPTER SEVEN

Exchange Traded Fund (ETF)

An ETF, or Exchange-Traded Fund, is a type of investment fund that trades on an exchange like a stock. ETFs are designed to track the performance of a particular index, such as the Nifty500, or a specific sector or asset class. An ETF is called an exchange-traded fund because it's traded on an exchange just like stocks are. The price of an ETF's shares will change throughout the trading day as the shares are bought and sold on the market. This is unlike mutual funds, which are not traded on an exchange, and which trade only once per day after the markets close. Additionally, ETFs tend to be more cost-effective and more liquid compared to mutual funds.An ETF is a marketable security, meaning it has a share price that allows it to be easily bought and sold on exchanges throughout the day, and it can be sold short.

Here are some key features of ETFs:

Diversification: ETFs are designed to provide investors with exposure to a diversified portfolio of stocks, bonds, or other assets, which can help reduce risk.

Low Cost: ETFs are generally low cost compared to actively managed mutual funds, since they typically have lower management fees and lower trading costs.

Liquidity: ETFs are bought and sold on an exchange, so they are generally more liquid than mutual funds, which can only be traded at the end of the day.

Transparency: Since ETFs are designed to track a specific index, the holdings of the ETF are usually disclosed on a daily basis, which provides transparency to investors.

Flexibility: ETFs can be bought and sold throughout the trading day, so investors can take advantage of intraday price movements.

Tax Efficiency: ETFs are generally more tax-efficient than mutual funds, since they typically have lower capital gains distributions.

Index ETFs: These are funds that are designed to track a specific index.

Fixed Income ETFs: These funds are designed to provide exposure to nearly every type of bond available.

ETFs are designed to provide exposure to a specific industry, such as oil, medicines, or high technology.

Commodity ETFs: These funds are designed to track the price of a certain commodity, such as gold, oil, or corn.

Leveraged ETFs: These funds are designed to employ leverage to boost returns.

Unlike most ETFs: which are designed to track an index, actively managed ETFs are aimed to outperform it.

ETNs are debt securities guaranteed by the creditworthiness of the issuing bank that was established to enable access to illiquid markets; they also have the added advantage of generating virtually no short-term capital gains taxes.

ETFs that let the investors trade volatility or get exposure to a specific investing strategy - such as currency carry or covered call writing, are examples of alternative investment ETFs.

Style ETFs: These funds are designed to mirror a specific investment style or market size focus, such as large-cap value or small-cap growth.

Foreign market ETFs: These funds are designed to monitor non-Indian markets such as Japan's Nikkei Index or Hong Kong's Hang Seng Index.

Inverse ETFs: These funds are designed to profit from a drop in the underlying market or index.

Trading transactions - Since they are traded like stocks, investors can place order types (e.g., limit orders or stop-loss orders) that mutual funds cannot.

Risks of ETFs :

However, there are several disadvantages to using ETFs, which include the following-

Trading costs: If you invest modest sums frequently, dealing directly with a fund company in a no-load fund may be less expensive.

Illiquidity: Some lightly traded ETFs have huge bid or ask spreads, which means you'll be buying at the spread's high price and selling at the spread's low price.

While ETFs often mirror their underlying index pretty closely, technical difficulties might cause variances.

Settlement dates: ETF sales will not be settled for two days after the transaction; this implies that, as the seller, your money from an ETF sale is theoretically unavailable to reinvest for two days.

Different types of Deals :

There are several different types of deals that can take place in the stock market. Here are some of the most common types:

Market order: This is the most common type of order, in which an investor instructs a broker to buy or sell a specific number of shares at the current market price. The transaction is executed as soon as possible.

Limit order: With a limit order, an investor sets a specific price at which they want to buy or sell shares. The order is executed only if the stock reaches the desired price.

Stop order: A stop order is used to limit losses. With a stop order, an investor sets a price at which they want to sell shares if the stock drops to a certain level. The order is executed automatically if the stock reaches that price.

Stop limit order: This is a combination of a stop order and a limit order. An investor sets a price at which they want to sell shares if the stock drops to a certain level, but the order will only be executed if the stock reaches that price and then begins to rise again.

Market on close order: This type of order is executed at the end of the trading day, at the closing price.

Market on open order: This type of order is executed at the beginning of the trading day, at the opening price.

Good-til-cancelled order: With this type of order, an investor sets a specific price at which they want to buy or sell shares, and the order remains active until it is filled or cancelled.

Day order: A day order is only valid for the current trading day. If the order is not filled by the end of the day, it is automatically cancelled.

A block deal is a type of trade that involves a large quantity of securities being bought or sold by a single trader or a group of traders. This type of trade is usually conducted off the exchange, meaning that it does not take place on the open market. Instead, the buyer and seller agree on a price for the securities being traded, and the transaction is executed privately between the parties involved.

Block deals are typically used by institutional investors, such as mutual funds, hedge funds, and pension funds, who are looking to buy or sell a large quantity of securities in a single transaction. By executing a block deal, these investors can avoid the potential price impact of their trades on the open market, which could otherwise result in unfavorable prices.

Block deals are subject to certain regulations and disclosure requirements, and they are typically reported to the exchange after they have been executed. In some cases, block deals may also be used to facilitate mergers and acquisitions or other corporate transactions, where a large block of shares may be traded as part of the deal.

A bulk deal refers to a transaction where a large quantity of goods or securities are bought or sold in a single transaction. Bulk deals are usually made between institutional investors, such as mutual funds, pension funds, and hedge funds.

In the case of securities, a bulk deal usually involves a single transaction of a significant number of shares of a company's stock. The transaction must be reported to the stock exchange where the stock is traded. This is because such a transaction can have a significant impact on the market price of the security, and the stock exchange needs to ensure that there is transparency and fairness in the trading of the stock.

Sector or Industry Analysis :

Sector or Industry analysis is the process of evaluating the performance and potential of a specific sector or industry, typically for investment or business planning purposes. This analysis involves examining the key economic and market factors that affect the sector or industry, such as trends, competition, regulation, and technology.

The main purpose of sector or industry analysis is to gain insights into the overall health and prospects of a particular sector or industry, which can inform investment decisions or strategic planning for businesses operating in that sector. **Some of the key components of sector or industry analysis include:**

Market Size and Growth: An assessment of the size of the sector or industry and its projected growth rate over a certain period.

Competition: An evaluation of the competitive landscape and the market share held by key players in the sector or industry.

Regulatory Environment: An analysis of the regulatory environment that governs the sector or industry, including laws and policies that affect its operations.

Technology: An assessment of the impact of technology on the sector or industry, including new innovations, trends, and disruptions.

Supply Chain and Distribution: An evaluation of the supply chain and distribution networks that support the sector or industry, including any vulnerabilities or strengths.

By analyzing these factors and other relevant data, investors or businesses can make informed decisions about investing in or operating in a particular sector or industry.

Key Notes 1:

- **Never buy any stock just it ia a low price only buy when there is up reversal or bounceback**
- **Pyramid or trade systematically**
- **Decrease your trading after a series of succeess full traders.**
- **Dont change your opinion during Market hours untill not shoing on chart confirmation.**
- **Dont follow the crowd or herd untill not exprirnce that self because a coin has two aspects.**

CHAPTER EIGHT

Technical Analysis

Technical analysis is a method of analyzing financial markets that involves studying past price and volume data to identify patterns, trends, and potential trading opportunities. Technical analysts use charts and other tools to visually represent market data and look for signals that indicate whether a security or market is likely to rise or fall in the future.

Technical analysis is based on the idea that market prices reflect all available information, including fundamental factors like economic indicators and company financials, as well as psychological and behavioral factors like investor sentiment and market momentum. By analyzing price trends and patterns, technical analysts aim to gain insight into these underlying factors and make informed predictions about future market movements.

Common technical analysis tools include moving averages, trend lines, support and resistance levels, and various technical indicators like relative strength index (RSI), moving average convergence divergence (MACD), and stochastic oscillators. Traders use these tools to identify buying and selling signals and to determine optimal entry and exit points for their trades.

While technical analysis is a popular approach among traders and investors, it has its limitations. Critics argue that it is based on subjective interpretations of market data and may be influenced by market noise and other random factors. As with any investment strategy, it is important to conduct thorough research and analysis before making trading decisions.

Technical analysis is the study of historical market data, primarily price and volume, to identify patterns, trends, and potential trading opportunities. There are various tools and techniques used in technical analysis to help traders make informed trading decisions. Here are some of the most popular technical analysis tools:

- **Moving Averages**: A moving average is a trend-following indicator that smooths out price data by calculating an average of the price over a certain period of time. It helps traders identify the direction of the trend and potential support and resistance levels.
- **Relative Strength Index** (RSI): The RSI is a momentum oscillator that measures the speed and change of price movements. It indicates when an asset is overbought or oversold, and can be used to identify potential trend reversals.
- **Fibonacci Retracement**: The Fibonacci retracement tool is used to identify potential support and resistance levels based on the Fibonacci sequence. Traders use this tool to identify areas where the price is likely to reverse or continue a trend.
- **Bollinger Bands**: Bollinger Bands are volatility indicators that consist of three lines - a simple moving average and upper and lower bands that are placed two standard deviations away from the moving average. They help traders identify potential breakouts and the volatility of an asset.
- **Candlestick charts**: Candlestick charts are a popular way to represent price movements. They display the open, high, low, and close prices of an asset for a specific period, and use different colored candles to indicate bullish or bearish sentiment.
- **Moving Average Convergence Divergence** (MACD): The MACD is a trend-following momentum indicator that uses moving averages to identify potential trend reversals. It consists of two lines - a fast and slow moving average - and a histogram that indicates the difference between the two.
- **Volume**: Volume is a key component of technical analysis. It measures the number of shares or contracts that are traded in a specific period and is used to confirm price movements and identify potential trend reversals.

These are just a few of the many technical analysis tools available to traders. Each tool has its own strengths and weaknesses, and traders often use a combination of tools to make informed trading decisions.

Line Chart

Chart reading is a technique used in stock market analysis that involves examining the price movement of a particular stock over a period of time. The goal of chart reading is to identify patterns and trends in the stock's price history in order to make informed trading decisions.

To read a stock chart, you will typically need to do the following:

Choose a time frame: Stock charts can be viewed over a range of time frames, from minutes to years. The time frame you choose will depend on your investment goals and trading strategy.

Identify the trend: Look for trends in the stock's price movement, such as whether it's been trending up or down, or if it's been trading in a range.

Spot key **support and resistance levels**: Support and resistance levels are areas on a stock chart where the price has historically bounced off of, either in an upward or downward trend. These levels can be used to help make trading decisions, such as where to set stop-loss orders or where to enter or exit a trade.

Use technical indicators: Technical indicators are mathematical calculations based on a stock's price and/or volume that can help provide additional insights into the stock's behavior. Examples of technical indicators include moving averages, MACD, and RSI.

Analyze trading volume: **Trading volume** refers to the number of shares of a stock that are traded over a given period of time. High volume can indicate strong interest in a stock, while low volume may suggest that investors are less interested in the stock.

Overall, chart reading can be a useful tool in analyzing stocks, but it is important to remember that it is only one part of a larger investment strategy. It is important to combine chart analysis with other types of research and analysis, such as fundamental analysis, to make informed trading decisions.

Demand & Supply:

In stock markets, the forces of supply and demand determine the prices of stocks. **The supply of a stock** refers to the total number of shares that are available for sale, while demand refers to the total number of shares that buyers are willing to purchase at a given price.

If there is high demand for a stock, and the supply is low, then the price of the stock is likely to increase. Conversely, if there is low demand for a stock, and the supply is high, then the price is likely to decrease.

The price of a stock is also influenced by various other factors, such as the overall performance of the company, the economic conditions, and the news and events that affect the industry or sector the company operates in.

Investors and traders use various technical and fundamental analysis techniques to analyze the supply and demand dynamics of a stock and make decisions about buying or selling the stock. Understanding the supply and demand dynamics is an important aspect of investing in the stock market.

Price & Volume :

Price and volume analysis is a method used to evaluate the behavior of an asset, such as a stock or a commodity, based on its price movements and trading volume. The analysis involves examining charts that plot the asset's historical price and volume data to identify trends, patterns, and potential trading opportunities.

Price analysis focuses on identifying the various levels of support and resistance, which represent areas where the price may encounter buying or selling pressure. Technical analysts use various indicators such as moving averages, oscillators, and chart patterns to identify potential buy or sell signals. For instance, if the price breaks through a resistance level with high volume, it may signal a bullish trend, while a break below a support level with high volume may signal a bearish trend.

Volume analysis, on the other hand, involves examining the trading volume of an asset to identify trends and potential changes in market sentiment. High trading volume typically accompanies price movements, and it can be used to confirm the strength or weakness of a trend. For example, a high volume breakout from a trading range can suggest that the price may continue to trend in that direction, while low volume during a price movement may indicate a lack of conviction in the trend.

Price and volume analysis can be used by traders and investors to make informed decisions about buying or selling an asset. However, it is important to remember that past price and volume trends do not necessarily guarantee future performance, and other factors such as market news, economic data, and geopolitical events can also influence the price and volume of an asset.

Support & Resistance :

Support and resistance levels are key concepts in technical analysis, which is the study of past price and volume data to forecast future market movements. These levels represent price levels where the market has historically shown a tendency to reverse direction, either because buyers (support) or sellers (resistance) have stepped in to influence the price.

A support level is a price level at which there is a significant concentration of demand for a particular asset. Traders and investors often use this level as an entry point to buy the asset, believing that the market is likely to rise from this point.

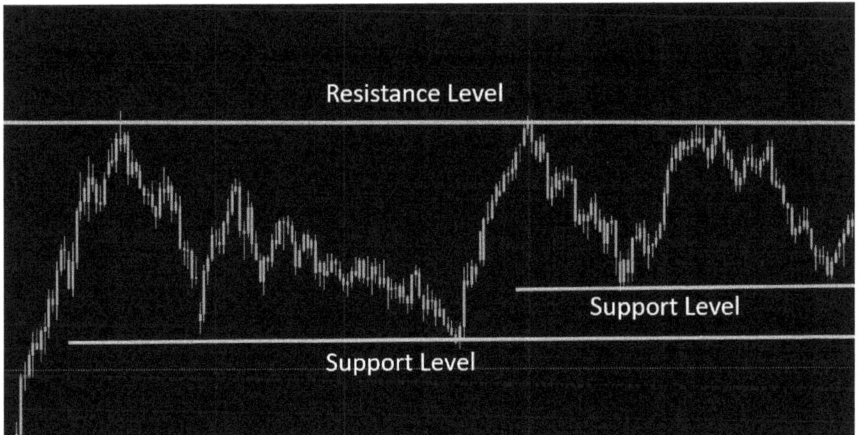

Support and Resistance

A resistance level is a price level at which there is a significant concentration of supply for a particular asset. Traders and investors often use this level as an exit point to sell the asset, believing that the market is likely to fall from this point.

Breakouts occur when the price of an asset moves through a significant support or resistance level. A breakout through a resistance level is seen as a bullish signal, as it suggests that the market is likely to continue its upward trend. Similarly, a breakout through a support level is seen as a bearish signal, as it suggests that the market is likely to continue its downward trend.

Traders often look for breakout opportunities as a way to profit from significant price movements in the market. However, it's important to note that breakouts can also result in false signals, where the price briefly moves through a support or resistance level before quickly reversing direction. As with all technical analysis tools, it's important to use other indicators and analysis methods to confirm the validity of breakout signals.

Trend :

In the stock market, a trend refers to the general direction in which a particular stock or the overall market is moving. Trends can be upward, downward, or sideways.

An **upward trend**, also known as a bullish trend, refers to a sustained period of time where the market or a particular stock is generally increasing in value. This is usually seen as a positive sign for investors, as it suggests that the stock or market is performing well.

A **downward trend**, also known as a bearish trend, refers to a sustained period of time where the market or a particular stock is generally decreasing in value. This is usually seen as a negative sign for investors, as it suggests that the stock or market is performing poorly.

A **sideways trend**, also known as a consolidation trend, refers to a period of time where the stock or the market is moving within a narrow range without a clear direction. This can be frustrating for investors who are looking for clear signals to buy or sell.

Trends are often used by traders and investors to make decisions about buying or selling stocks. Technical analysts study the patterns and trends in stock prices to predict future movements and make investment decisions based on these predictions.

Time Frame :

The term "time frame" in the context of stock usually refers to the length of time over which an investor plans to hold a particular stock or make trading decisions.

Investors may have different time frames depending on their investment objectives, risk tolerance, and market outlook. Some investors may prefer short-term time frames, such as day trading or swing trading, where they buy and sell stocks within a few hours or days. Other investors may have a long-term time frame, where they buy and hold stocks for years or even decades, with the aim of benefiting from the long-term growth potential of the companies they invest in.

The time frame chosen by an investor is often based on their investment goals and risk tolerance. Short-term traders may be seeking to make quick profits from market volatility, while long-term investors may be seeking to accumulate wealth over a longer period of time.

It's important to note that no single time frame is right for everyone, and investors should choose a time frame that aligns with their investment goals, risk tolerance, and overall investment strategy.

Day trading typically refers to the practice of buying and selling securities within the same trading day. In general, day traders aim to make profits from short-term price movements in the market.

The time frame for day trading can vary depending on a trader's strategy and personal preferences, but it typically involves opening and closing positions within the same trading day. Some day traders may hold positions for only a few minutes, while others may hold them for several hours.

Many day traders focus on the first hour or two of the trading day when there is typically higher volatility and more price movement. Others may choose to trade during specific market hours, such as when the US markets overlap with the European markets, in order to take advantage of increased trading volume and liquidity.

It's worth noting that day trading can be a high-risk activity and requires a significant amount of skill, knowledge, and discipline. It's important to thoroughly research and understand the risks involved before engaging in day trading.

The time frame for swing trading can vary depending on the individual trader's strategy and goals, but typically it involves holding positions for a few days to a few weeks. Swing traders aim to capture short-term price movements and may use technical analysis to identify trends and patterns in the market.

Some swing traders may hold positions for a shorter time frame, such as a few hours or a day, while others may hold positions for longer, up to several months. The key is to hold positions long enough to capture a significant price movement, but not so long that the trade becomes a long-term investment.

Ultimately, the time frame for swing trading depends on the trader's risk tolerance, trading style, and market conditions. It's important to have a well-defined strategy and plan for entering and exiting trades, as well as managing risk.

Moving Average :

A moving average is a widely used statistical tool that helps to smooth out fluctuations in a time series data by taking the average of a certain number of past observations. It is a simple yet effective technique that is often used in finance, economics, and other fields to analyze trends, identify patterns, and make predictions.

Moving Average

There are several types of moving averages, but the most commonly used ones are the simple moving average (SMA) and the exponential moving average (EMA). The SMA is calculated by adding up the prices of an asset over a certain number of periods and then dividing by the number of periods. The EMA, on the other hand, gives more weight to recent prices by using a smoothing factor.

Moving averages can be plotted on a chart to visualize the trend in the data. Traders and analysts often use moving averages as a trading signal, where they look for crossovers between short-term and long-term moving averages to indicate a change in trend.

There are many tools available online and in trading software that allow you to calculate and plot moving averages on a chart. These tools can be customized with different settings, such as the number of periods and the type of moving average, to fit the user's needs.

A 200-50 moving average refers to a technical analysis indicator used in finance and trading. It is calculated by taking the average of the closing prices of an asset over the last 50 days and the last 200 days.

The 200-day moving average is considered a long-term trend indicator, while the 50-day moving average is a short-term trend indicator. When the shorter-term moving average (50-day) crosses above the longer-term moving average (200-day), it is considered a bullish signal indicating that the asset's price is likely to continue rising. On the other hand, when the 50-day moving average crosses below the 200-day moving average, it is considered a bearish signal indicating that the asset's price is likely to continue falling.

Traders and investors use this indicator to help identify trends and potential entry and exit points for trades. However, it's important to note that moving averages should not be used in isolation and should be used in conjunction with other technical analysis indicators and fundamental analysis to make informed trading decisions.

MACD stands for Moving Average Convergence Divergence. It is a technical analysis indicator used to identify changes in a security's trend.

MACD is calculated by subtracting the 26-period exponential moving average (EMA) from the 12-period EMA. A 9-period EMA, called the "signal line," is then plotted on top of the MACD line, which can help traders identify potential buy or sell signals.

When the MACD line crosses above the signal line, it can be interpreted as a bullish signal, indicating that the security's momentum is starting to shift upwards. Conversely, when the MACD line crosses below the signal line, it can be interpreted as a bearish signal, indicating that the security's momentum is starting to shift downwards.

Traders also pay attention to the divergence between the MACD line and the price of the security. If the price of the security is moving in one direction, but the MACD line is moving in the opposite direction, it can be a sign of a potential trend reversal.

MACD

It's important to note that like all technical analysis indicators, MACD should be used in conjunction with other forms of analysis to make informed trading decisions.

RSI stands for Relative Strength Index, which is a technical analysis indicator used to measure the strength or weakness of a stock or other financial asset. The RSI indicator is used to identify overbought or oversold conditions in the market, and is typically calculated using the closing prices of a stock over a specified time period.

The RSI indicator is calculated using the following formula:

RSI = 100 - (100 / (1 + RS))

Where RS (Relative Strength) is calculated as the average gain of up periods divided by the average loss of down periods over the specified time period. The RSI value ranges from 0 to 100, with values above 70 indicating overbought conditions and values below 30 indicating oversold conditions.

Traders and investors use the RSI indicator to identify potential trend reversals or entry and exit points for trades. However, it is important to note that like any technical indicator, the RSI should not be used in isolation and should be combined with other forms of analysis to make informed trading decisions.

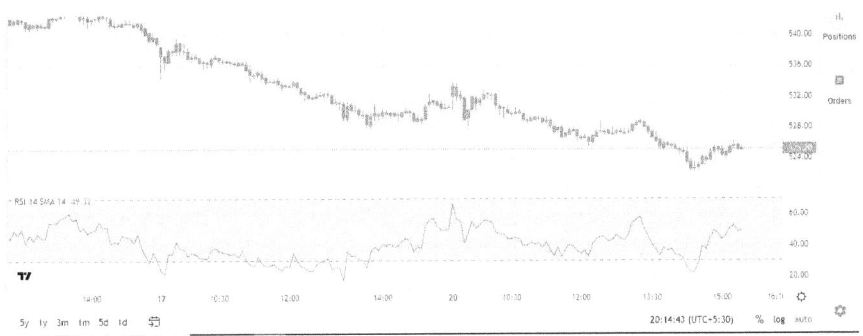

RSI

The Average Directional Index (ADX) is a technical analysis indicator that is used to measure the strength of a trend. It was developed by J. Welles Wilder in the late 1970s.

The ADX indicator consists of three lines: the ADX line, the positive directional indicator (+DI) line, and the negative directional indicator (-DI) line. The ADX line represents the overall strength of the trend, while the +DI and -DI lines represent the upward and downward movements of the asset price, respectively.

ADX

The ADX line typically oscillates between 0 and 100. A reading below 20 indicates a weak trend, while a reading above 40 indicates a strong trend.

Traders may use the ADX indicator to help determine whether a market is trending or ranging. Additionally, they may use the +DI and -DI lines to help identify potential buy and sell signals. For example, if the +DI line crosses above the -DI line, it may be a bullish signal, while a cross below may be a bearish signal.

Bollinger Bands are a technical analysis tool used to measure a security's volatility and to identify potential overbought or oversold conditions. Developed by John Bollinger in the 1980s, Bollinger Bands consist of three lines:

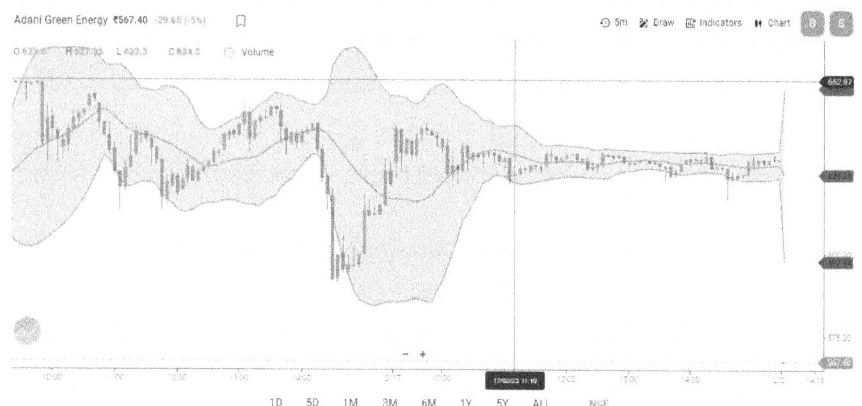

Bollinger Band

The middle band, which is a simple moving average (SMA) of the security's price over a certain number of periods.

The upper band, which is the middle band plus a specified number of standard deviations of the security's price over the same number of periods.

The lower band, which is the middle band minus the same number of standard deviations.

The most common number of periods used for the calculation is 20, and the standard deviation multiplier is typically set at 2. The width of the bands adjusts according to the volatility of the security, with wider bands indicating higher volatility and narrower bands indicating lower volatility.

Traders use Bollinger Bands to identify potential entry and exit points for trades. When the price of a security reaches the upper band, it may be overbought, indicating that it is trading at a higher price than it should be based on its fundamentals. When the price reaches the lower band, it may be oversold, indicating that it is trading at a lower price than it should be. These conditions may be used to identify potential buy or sell signals. Additionally, traders may watch for price breakouts above or below the bands as a signal that the security's price is likely to continue moving in the same direction.

VWAP stands for Volume Weighted Average Price. It is a trading benchmark used by traders and investors to assess the overall market trend and help them make trading decisions.

VWAP

VWAP is calculated by taking the sum of the price multiplied by the trading volume for each transaction in a given trading day and dividing it by the total trading volume for that day. The result is the average price at which all shares were traded for that day, weighted by their respective trading volumes.

Traders use VWAP as a reference point to compare the current market price of a security to its average price for the day. If the current price is above the VWAP, it suggests that the security is overpriced, and if it is below the VWAP, it suggests that the security is underpriced.

VWAP is especially popular in algorithmic trading as it can help traders identify optimal times to enter or exit a trade based on whether the current market price is above or below the VWAP.

A candlestick chart : A candlestick chart is a type of financial chart used to represent the price movement of an asset, such as a stock, commodity, or currency pair, over a specific period of time. The chart is composed of individual "candles" that indicate the open, high, low, and close prices for each period.

Each candle represents a specified time frame, such as one day, one hour, or one minute. The body of the candle represents the opening and closing prices for the period, and the wicks or shadows above and below the body represent the highest and lowest prices reached during that time.

A candlestick chart is useful for traders and investors as it provides a visual representation of the price movements over time and can help identify trends and potential buy or sell signals. By analyzing the patterns and formations of the candles, traders can make more informed decisions about when to enter or exit a trade. Some common candlestick patterns include dojis, hammers, shooting stars, and engulfing patterns.

Candlestick charts are a popular tool used in technical analysis to track and analyze the movement of financial assets such as stocks, bonds, currencies, and commodities. There are several types of candlestick charts, each with their unique features and significance. Here are some of the most common types:

Marubozu: This is a candlestick chart with no shadows or wicks, indicating that the opening price was the same as the closing price. A bullish marubozu is formed when the closing price is higher than the opening price, while a bearish marubozu is formed when the closing price is lower than the opening price.

Doji: A doji is a candlestick with a small body and long wicks on both ends, indicating indecision in the market. A bullish doji is formed when the opening price is the same as the closing price but lower than the highest price of the day, while a bearish doji is formed when the opening price is the same as the closing price but higher than the lowest price of the day.

Hammer: A hammer is a candlestick with a small body, a long lower wick, and little or no upper wick, indicating a potential bullish reversal. A bullish hammer is formed when the closing price is higher than the opening price but lower than the highest price of the day.

Shooting Star: A shooting star is a candlestick with a small body, a long upper wick, and little or no lower wick, indicating a potential bearish reversal. A bearish shooting star is formed when the closing price is lower than the opening price but higher than the lowest price of the day.

Spinning Top: A spinning top is a candlestick with a small body and long upper and lower wicks, indicating indecision in the market. It can be a bullish or bearish reversal signal depending on the price action that follows.

Engulfing: An engulfing candlestick is formed when a small candlestick is followed by a larger candlestick that completely engulfs the previous one. A bullish engulfing pattern is formed when the second candlestick is green and the first is red, while a bearish engulfing pattern is formed when the second candlestick is red and the first is green.

Dark Cloud Cover: A dark cloud cover is a bearish reversal pattern formed when a bullish candlestick is followed by a bearish candlestick that opens above the previous day's high and closes below the midpoint of the previous day's candlestick.

These are just a few of the many types of candlestick charts used in technical analysis. Traders and investors use these charts to identify potential trading opportunities and make informed decisions based on the price action of financial assets.

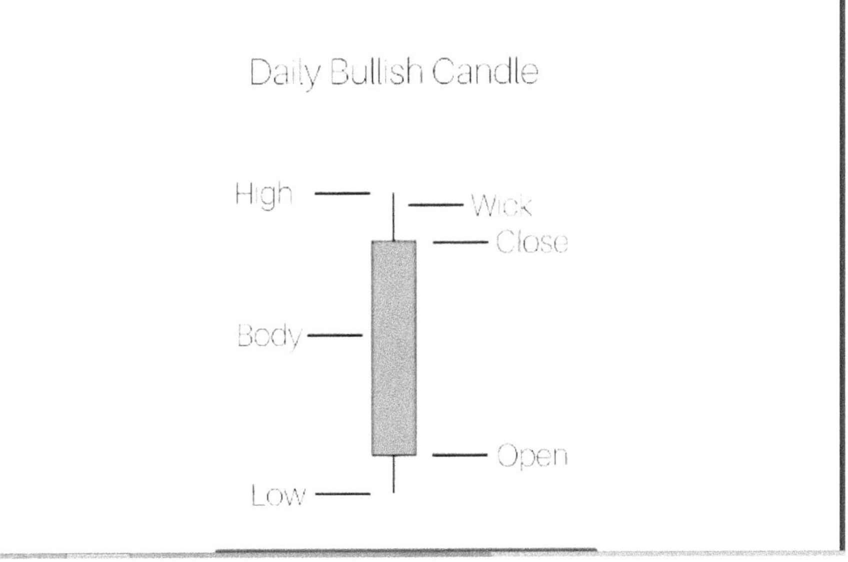

Anatomy of candle Stick

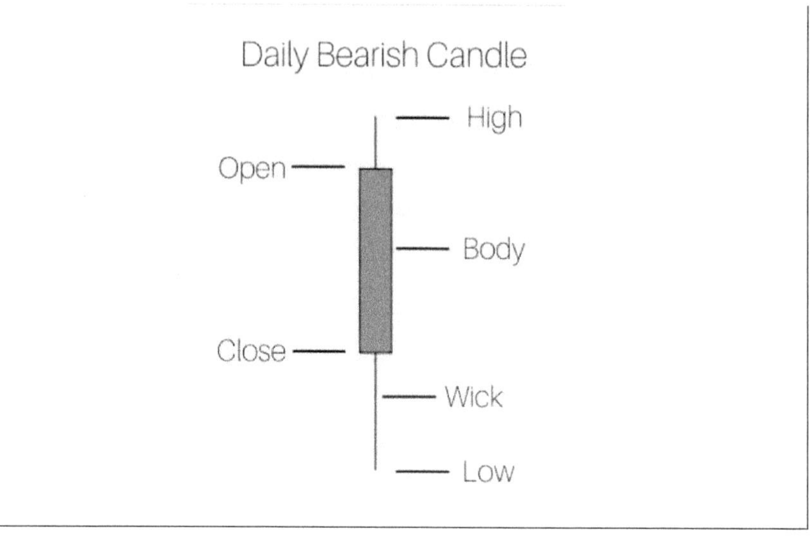

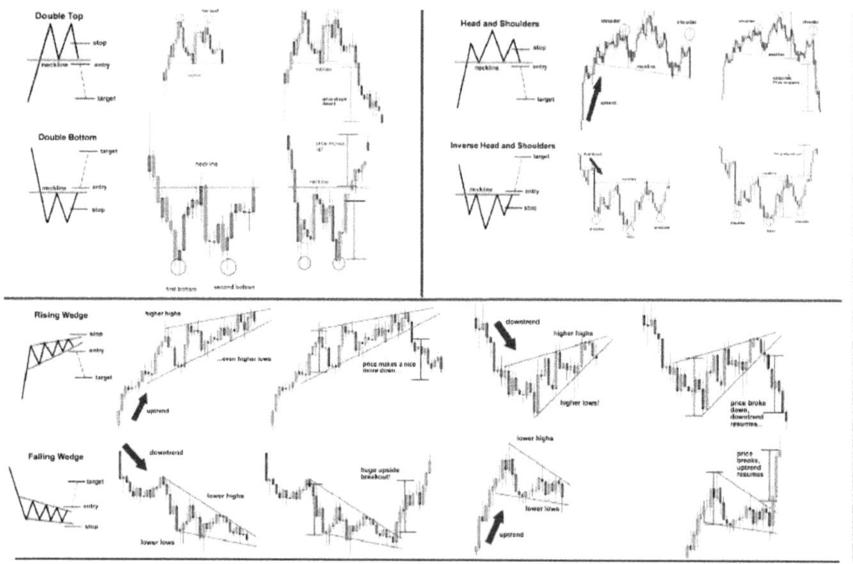

Reversal Chart Pattern

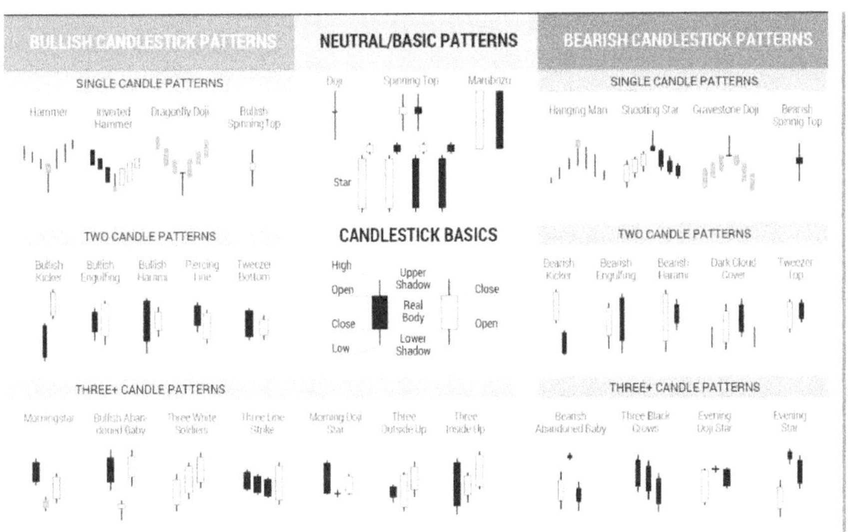
BULLISH CANDLESTICK PATTERNS
NEUTRAL/BASIC PATTERNS
BEARISH CANDLESTICK PATTERNS
SINGLE CANDLE PATTERNS
Hammer
Inverted Hammer
Dragonfly Doji
Bullish Spinning Top
Doji
Spinning Top
Marubozu
Star
SINGLE CANDLE PATTERNS
Hanging Man
Shooting Star
Gravestone Doji
Bearish Spinnig Top
TWO CANDLE PATTERNS
Bullish Kicker
Bullish Engulfing
Bullish Harami
Piercing Line
Tweezer Bottom
CANDLESTICK BASICS
High
Open
Close
Low
Upper Shadow
Real Body
Lower Shadow
Close
Open
TWO CANDLE PATTERNS
Bearish Kicker
Bearish Engulfing
Bearish Harami
Dark Cloud Cover
Tweezer Top
THREE+ CANDLE PATTERNS
Morningstar
Bullish Abandoned Baby
Three White Soldiers
Three Line Strike
Morning Doji Star
Three Outside Up
Three Inside Up
THREE+ CANDLE PATTERNS
Bearish Abandoned Baby
Three Black Crows
Evening Doji Star
Evening Star

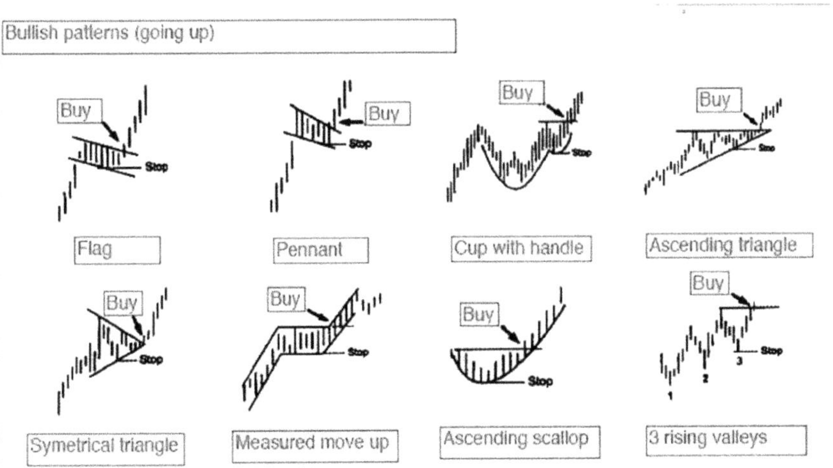
Bullish patterns (going up)
Buy
Stop
Flag
Buy
Stop
Pennant
Buy
Stop
Cup with handle
Buy
Stop
Ascending triangle
Buy
Stop
Symetrical triangle
Buy
Stop
Measured move up
Buy
Stop
Ascending scallop
Buy
Stop
1
2
3
3 rising valleys

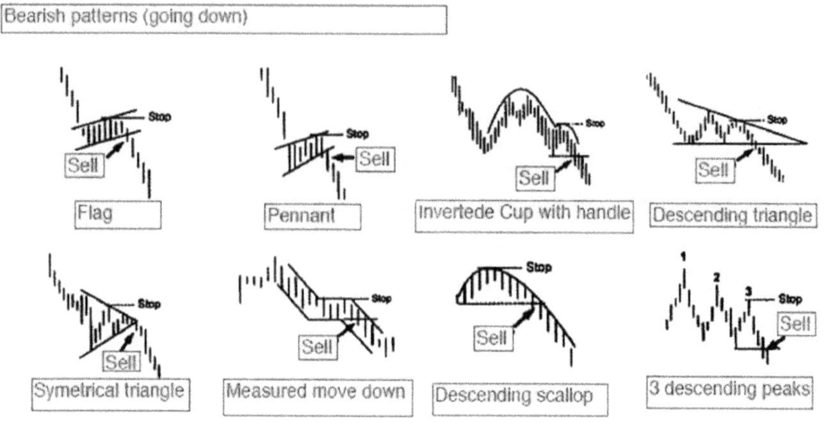

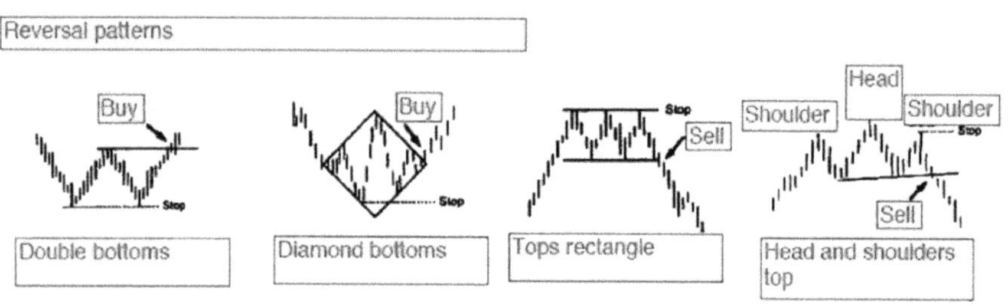

Enter Caption

What is the Horizontal Line?

A Horizontal Line shows the horizontal level in the chart. It can act as both Support and Resistance levels. Moreover, with the use of a horizontal level or line, you can easily decide whether you should exit a trade. That's because the horizontal level in the chart can help you figure out where a change is going to take place in the trend.

How to draw a horizontal line?

First, you need to spot a past price-level where the price had difficulties to break above or below.

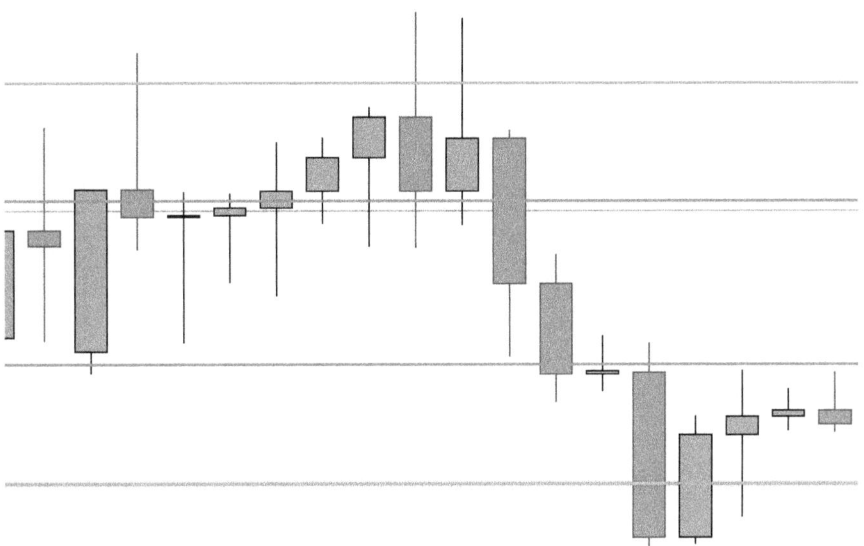

Horizontal Line

Then mark it with a horizontal line and Adjust it so that you get the highest number of touches (whether it's body or wick).

Once the price approaches this horizontal line again, there is a high chance that the price will retrace from that line.

What is a Trend line?

TREND LINE : Just like a horizontal line, there is a trend line and the only difference is a trend line is in a sloping direction

There are two types of trend lines

Upward Trend Line: "Sloping" area on the chart that shows upward buying pressure.

Downward Trend Line: "Sloping" area on the chart that shows downward selling pressure.

How to draw a trendline?

First, you need to spot an angle either upwards or downwards where you can see the price has taken support or had a resistance

Start drawing a line from the lowest candle

Adjust it so that you get the highest number of touches(whether it's a body or a wick)

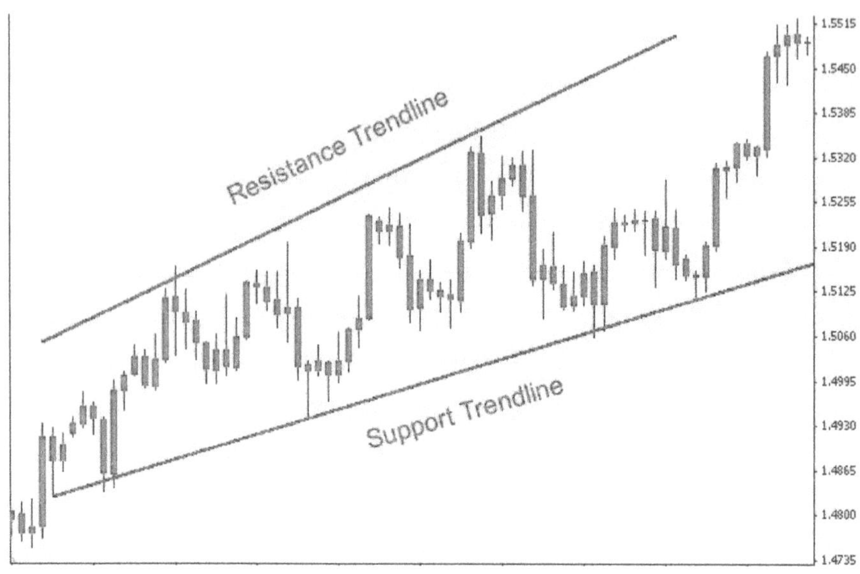

Trend Line

Heikin-Ashi : Heikin-Ashi is a Japanese trading indicator and financial chart that means "average pace". Heikin-Ashi charts resemble candlestick charts, but have a smoother appearance as they track a range of price movements, rather than tracking every price movement as with candlesticks

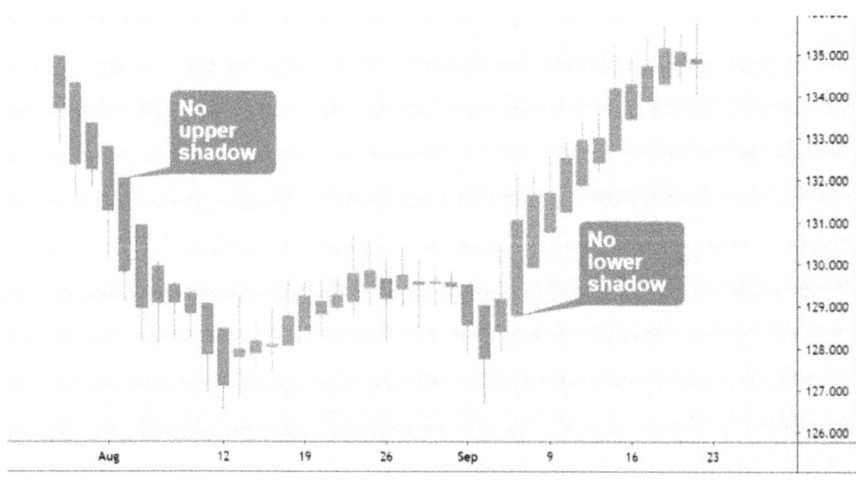

Heikin Ashi

The Fibonacci : The Fibonacci retracement tool plots percentage retracement lines based upon the mathematical relationship within the Fibonacci sequence. These retracement levels provide support and resistance levels that can be used to target price objectives.

Fibonacci Retracements are displayed by first drawing a trend line between two extreme points. A series of six horizontal lines are drawn intersecting the trend line at the Fibonacci levels of 0.0%, 23.6%, 38.2%, 50%, 61.8%, and 100%.

Fibonacci

Pivot pointIn financial markets, a pivot point is a price level that is used by traders as a possible indicator of market movement. A pivot point is calculated as an average of significant prices from the performance of a market in the prior trading period

Pivot Point

Key notes :

- Keep your chart up to date
- Dont follow only chart price and volume are very important in it.
- Preserve your capital your always should target to save capital and earn profit.
- Markets are never wrong opinion may be
- Practice chart and learn from your mistakes

CHAPTER NINE

Future & options

Futures and options are financial derivatives that allow investors to speculate on the future price movements of underlying assets.

Futures: A futures contract is an agreement between two parties to buy or sell an underlying asset at a specific price and time in the future. Futures contracts are traded on exchanges and are standardized in terms of quantity, quality, delivery date, and delivery location. The two parties to the contract agree to buy or sell the underlying asset at the specified price on the delivery date. Futures contracts are used to hedge against price fluctuations, speculate on price movements, and to arbitrage between different markets.

Options: An option is a contract that gives the holder the right, but not the obligation, to buy or sell an underlying asset at a specified price on or before a specified date. The buyer of an option pays a premium to the seller for the right to buy or sell the underlying asset at the specified price. The seller of the option is obligated to sell or buy the underlying asset if the buyer chooses to exercise the option. There are two types of options: call options and put options. A call option gives the holder the right to buy the underlying asset, while a put option gives the holder the right to sell the underlying asset.

Options are used for hedging against price fluctuations, generating income through selling options, and speculating on price movements. Options can also be used in combination with other financial instruments to create complex trading strategies.

Both futures and options are leveraged instruments, meaning that traders can control a large amount of the underlying asset with a relatively small amount of capital. However, this also means that losses can be magnified if the price movements go against the trader's position.

Futures & Options

MARKET OPENS IN 3 DAYS

Option Chains

NIFTY 50	17,844.60	BANKNIFTY	40,701.70	FINNIFTY	18,252.55
NSE	-99.60 (0.56%)	NSE	-430.05 (1.05%)	NSE	-181.55 (0.98%)

Index Options Top Traded

BANKNIFTY 41000 Put	BANKNIFTY 40500 Put	NIFTY 18000 Call	NIFTY 17900 Put
23 Feb '23	23 Feb '23	23 Feb '23	23 Feb '23
₹382.40	₹146.00	₹37.00	₹101.00
160.45 (72.29%)	57.10 (64.23%)	-35.90 (-49.25%)	27.05 (36.58%)

Nifty

In summary, futures and options are financial instruments that allow investors to speculate on the future price movements of underlying assets. Both futures and options are used for hedging, income generation, and speculation, but they carry a higher level of risk due to the use of leverage.

"Call" and "put" options are types of financial contracts that give the holder the right, but not the obligation, to buy or sell an underlying asset at a specified price (called the "strike price") on or before a specified date.

In the context of futures options, these are known as "futures call options" and "futures put options." A futures call option gives the holder the right to buy a futures contract at the strike price, while a futures put option gives the holder the right to sell a futures contract at the strike price.

Futures options are similar to stock options, but instead of buying or selling the underlying stock, the holder of a futures option is buying or selling a futures contract. A futures contract is an agreement to buy or sell an underlying asset (such as a commodity or financial instrument) at a specific price and date in the future.

Home > F&O > Option Chain

NIFTY 50 Option Chain Expiry 23 Feb 2023

OI (lots)	CALL PRICE	STRIKE PRICE	PUT PRICE	OI (lots)
773 +36.57%	₹324.80 -85.55 (20.85%)	17,550.00	₹9.00 -1.35 (13.04%)	41,686 +32.46%
14,340 +6.46%	₹282.00 -61.80 (22.48%)	17,600.00	₹13.15 [illegible]	1,21,671 +35.30%
1,686 +31.41%	₹236.00 -79.95 (25.30%)	17,650.00	₹19.10 [illegible]	55,670 [illegible]
18,020 +23.73%	₹194.20 -78.80 (28.86%)	17,700.00	₹28.00 [illegible]	98,288 [illegible]
7,624 +105.89%	₹157.50 -73.30 (31.76%)	17,750.00	₹39.00 [illegible]	34,614 -9.06%

Nifty

HERE ARE SOME KEY FEATURES OF THE CALL OPTION:

Specifics: To buy a 'call' option, you have to place a buy order with your broker specifying the strike price and the expiry date. You will also have to specify how much you are ready to pay for the call option.Fixed Price: The strike price for a call option is the fixed amount at which you agree to buy the underlying assets in the future. It is also known as the exercise price. Option Premium: When you buy the call option, you must pay the option writer a premium. This is first paid to the exchange, which then passes it on to the option seller.Margins: You sell call options by paying an initial margin, and not the entire sum. However, once you have paid the margin, you also have to maintain a minimum amount in your trading account or with your broker. Premium: Stock and Index Options: Depending on the underlying asset, there are two kinds of call options – Index options and Stock options. Option can only be exercised on the expiry date. While most of the traits are similar .

SQUARING OFF: In the case of Stock options, you can buy an opposing contract. This means, if you hold a contract to sell stocks, you purchase a contract to buy the very same stocks. This is called squaring off. You make a profit from the difference in prices and premiums.

Volatility of a stock refers to the degree of variation in the price of a stock over time. It is a statistical measure of the dispersion of returns for a given security or market index. In simple terms, it is the degree of fluctuation in the price of a stock in a given period of time.

The volatility of a stock is calculated by measuring the standard deviation of its returns over a certain period of time. High volatility means that the stock price can experience rapid and significant changes, while low volatility means that the price is relatively stable and predictable.

Investors often use volatility as an indicator of risk, as stocks with high volatility are considered riskier than those with low volatility. However, volatility can also provide opportunities for investors to make profits through trading strategies that take advantage of price movements.

Expiry : Monthly Future and Options Contra ct expiry day. Monthly Future and options contracts expire on every last Thursday of a month. If a trading holiday falls on the last Thursday, then the previous trading day will be the expiry day of the Futures and Options contracts

What are Options? Options are probably the best instrument to trade because, with the help of options, you can create a different view on markets simultaneously. For example, you can go long, and at the same time, you can go short for the same underlying asset. You can't do this in the future and in the equity market, and hence I feel that they limit our profit probabilities. it is important to know that the options are part of the Derivative Market; the value of options is derived from the other underlying securities, such as stocks. There are two types of options –

1) Call Options.

2) Put Options.

As in stocks, two parties are involved; one is a buyer, and the other is a seller. In the same way, there are two participants, those who buy the options are referred to as Options Buyers, and those who sell options are called Options Sellers/Option Writers.

1. **Call Options** – Call Options are nothing but a legal contract that gives the buyer a right but not an obligation to buy a particular asset at a particular price on a particular date (referred to as the expiry date)

If you are bullish on a particular underlying asset and think that it can go up until expiry, you can think of buying a Call Option. For buying a specific call option buyer pays a particular premium to the Option Seller.

That premium consists of various factors such as Theta, Alpha, Gamma, vega etc. Another term you should understand here is 'strike price.'

The strike price is the price at which a particular option can be exercised. The closer the stock price of your option from the spot, the more premium you have to pay for buying that option.

1. **Put Options** – Put Options are nothing but a legal contract that gives the buyer a right but not an obligation to sell a particular asset at a predetermined price on a particular date.

You can buy a put option when you have a bearish view on a particular asset. Like the call option, for buying a put option, the buyer pays a particular premium to the option seller. As the price of the underlying assets decreases, the prices of the put options increase.

What are ITM, OTM and ATM options?

It is important to know What are ITM, OTM & ATM options before doing options trading.

1. **ITM Options** – ITM stands for In The Money Option. For the call option, ITM means the underlying price is greater than the strike price & for the put option, the ITM option means the underlying price is less than the strike price.

For example, Suppose nifty is at 17000; then, in this case, the 16900 Call Option will be in the money Call Option, whereas the 17100 Put Option will be in the money Put Option. As an option buyer, you should always trade in the money options because there is a high probability of profit compared to Out of money or At money options.

2. **OTM Options**– OTM stands for Out of The Money. For the call option, OTM means the underlying price is less than the option's strike price, and for the Put option, the OTM option will be the one whose strike price is less than the underlying price.

For example, (Considering the previous example) Suppose nifty is at 17000, the 17100 CE will be out of the money call option, whereas 16900 put option will be Out of the money put option. All the out of the money options go to 0 on the expiry day.

3. **ATM Options** – ATM stands for At The Money. If the underlying price is equal to the strike price, then, in that case, we can say that it is an ATM option.

For example, If nifty is at 17000, then 17000 CE & 17000 PE will be called At The Money Options. Similar to OTM options, these options will also go to zero if the underlying asset expires at the exact price equal to that particular strike pri

Understand that your current trade is the outcome of random distributions

When you trade, there is always the possibility of losing money. Your task as a trader is to take a calculated stop loss or trail your stop loss and keep on securing your profits until the trend is your friend! I have observed that many traders, when they take a trade, and when it goes in their direction, they shift their stop loss to breakeven, which is the right thing to do because as a trader, you should always manage your downside. Still, when their stop loss gets triggered out, they get frustrated & they end up doing revenge trading, which is not at all a good thing. Here, you need to understand that the breakeven is much better than a loss.

Remove emotions from your trading system

This is probably the most challenging thing to do, but there is no turning back once you do that! As a trader, you have to constantly cross-check whether your next decision is taken emotionally or without emotions.

Out of emotions, traders commit several mistakes, such as moving your profit level further ahead. You should not do this; it's a good thing to do when the market is trending, but you should always consider price action before extending your profit target; you should not move your target based on your emotions because, in the end, you will end up booking smaller profits.

In case of stop losses, you need to be more strict as compared to profit targets. As I mentioned before, you should always move your stop loss in only one direction, "in the direction of your trend". Also, when you take a trade, and It goes slightly against you, don't exit in panic; allow the market to hit your stop loss because that is the right thing to do. These

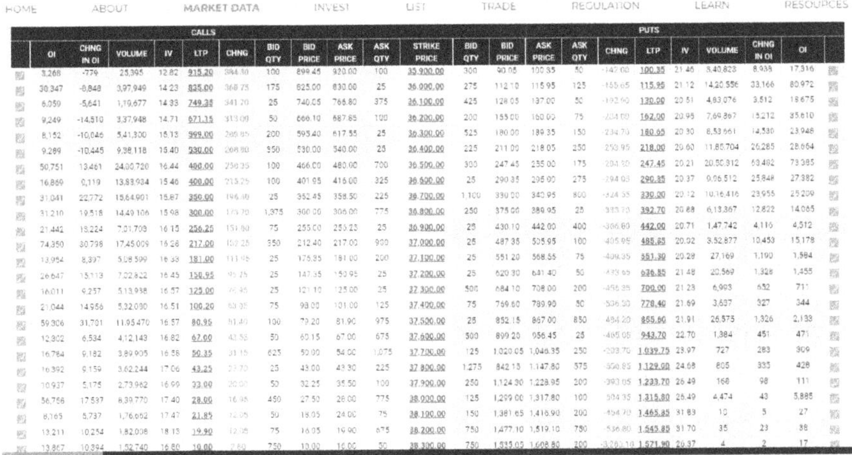
HOME ABOUT MARKET DATA INVEST LIST TRADE REGULATION LEARN RESOURCES

CALLS										STRIKE	PUTS									
OI	CHNG IN OI	VOLUME	IV	LTP	CHNG	BID QTY	BID PRICE	ASK PRICE	ASK QTY	STRIKE PRICE	BID QTY	BID PRICE	ASK PRICE	ASK QTY	CHNG	LTP	IV	VOLUME	CHNG IN OI	OI
3,268	-779	25,395	12.82	915.20	384.30	100	899.45	920.00	100	35,900.00	300	90.05	100.35	50	-142.00	100.35	21.46	8,40,823	8,938	17,316
30,347	-8,848	3,97,949	14.23	835.00	368.75	175	825.00	830.00	25	36,000.00	275	112.10	115.95	125	-155.65	115.95	21.12	14,20,556	33,166	80,972
6,059	-5,641	1,19,677	14.33	749.35	341.70	25	740.05	766.80	375	36,100.00	425	128.05	137.00	50	-192.90	130.00	20.51	4,83,076	3,512	18,675
9,249	-14,510	3,37,948	14.71	671.15	313.00	50	666.10	687.85	100	36,200.00	200	155.00	160.00	75	-204.00	162.00	20.95	7,69,867	15,212	35,610
8,152	-10,046	5,41,300	15.13	599.00	280.85	200	595.40	617.55	25	36,300.00	525	180.00	189.35	150	-234.70	180.65	20.30	8,53,661	14,530	23,946
9,289	-10,445	9,38,118	15.40	530.00	208.80	350	530.00	540.00	25	36,400.00	225	211.00	218.05	250	-253.95	218.00	20.60	11,85,704	26,285	28,664
50,751	13,461	24,00,720	16.44	480.00	250.35	100	466.00	480.00	700	36,500.00	300	247.45	255.00	175	-204.30	247.45	20.21	20,50,312	53,482	73,385
16,869	9,119	13,83,934	15.46	400.00	215.25	100	401.95	416.00	325	36,600.00	25	290.35	295.00	275	-294.05	290.35	20.37	9,06,512	25,848	27,382
31,041	22,772	15,64,901	15.87	350.00	196.40	25	352.45	358.50	225	36,700.00	1,100	330.00	340.95	800	-324.55	330.00	20.12	10,16,416	23,955	25,209
31,210	19,518	14,49,106	15.98	300.00	173.70	1,375	300.00	306.00	775	36,800.00	250	375.00	389.95	25	-333.70	392.70	20.88	6,13,367	12,822	14,065
21,442	18,224	7,01,709	16.15	256.25	151.80	75	255.00	256.23	25	36,900.00	25	430.10	442.00	400	-306.60	442.00	20.71	1,47,742	4,116	4,512
74,350	30,798	17,45,009	16.26	217.00	152.25	350	212.40	217.00	900	37,000.00	25	487.35	505.95	100	-405.95	485.85	20.02	3,52,877	10,453	15,178
13,954	8,397	5,08,599	16.33	181.00	111.95	25	175.35	181.00	200	37,100.00	25	551.20	568.55	75	-409.35	551.30	20.28	27,169	1,190	1,584
26,647	15,113	7,02,822	16.45	150.95	95.75	25	147.35	150.95	25	37,200.00	25	620.30	641.40	50	-433.65	636.85	21.48	20,569	1,328	1,455
16,011	9,257	5,13,938	16.57	125.00	76.95	25	121.10	125.00	25	37,300.00	500	684.10	708.00	200	-456.35	700.00	21.23	6,993	652	711
21,044	14,956	5,32,080	16.51	100.20	63.05	75	98.00	101.00	125	37,400.00	75	769.60	789.90	50	-536.30	778.40	21.69	3,637	327	344
59,306	31,701	11,95,470	16.57	80.95	51.40	100	79.20	81.90	975	37,500.00	25	852.15	867.00	850	-484.20	855.60	21.91	26,575	1,326	2,133
12,302	6,534	4,12,143	16.82	67.00	43.55	50	60.15	67.00	675	37,600.00	500	899.20	956.45	25	-465.05	943.70	22.70	1,384	451	471
16,784	9,182	3,89,905	16.58	50.35	31.15	625	50.00	54.00	1,075	37,700.00	125	1,020.05	1,046.35	250	-203.70	1,039.75	23.97	727	283	309
16,392	9,159	3,62,244	17.06	43.25	23.70	25	43.00	43.30	225	37,800.00	1,275	842.15	1,147.80	575	-350.85	1,129.00	24.68	805	335	428
10,937	5,175	2,73,962	16.99	33.00	20.00	50	32.25	35.50	100	37,900.00	250	1,124.30	1,228.95	200	-393.05	1,233.70	26.49	168	98	111
56,756	17,537	8,39,770	17.40	28.00	16.95	450	27.50	28.00	775	38,000.00	125	1,299.00	1,317.80	100	-504.35	1,315.80	26.49	4,474	43	5,885
8,165	5,737	1,76,662	17.47	21.85	12.05	50	18.05	24.00	75	38,100.00	150	1,381.65	1,416.90	200	-454.70	1,465.85	31.89	10	5	27
13,211	10,254	1,82,008	18.13	19.90	12.05	75	16.05	19.90	675	38,200.00	750	1,477.10	1,519.10	750	-536.80	1,545.85	31.70	35	23	38
13,867	10,394	1,52,740	16.80	10.00	7.60	750	10.00	16.00	50	38,300.00	750	1,535.05	1,608.80	200	-3,263.10	1,571.90	26.37	4	2	17

FNO

What is Butterfly Options Strategy?

The Butterfly Strategy is a neutral strategy that can be deployed using bullish and bearish spreads. While deploying this strategy, we short and buy options with the same expiration date.

Here are different types of butterfly spreads-

1.Long Call Butterfly Strategy

In this strategy, the trader has to buy one in the money call option, short two at the money call options, and buy one out of the money call option. This is a net debit strategy.

The maximum profit by initiating this strategy will occur when the index expires at the same strike price equal to the strike price of short calls

The maximum loss that can occur in this strategy will be the cost of the premiums paid plus taxes and brokerage.

2.Short Call Butterfly

This strategy is exactly the opposite of long call butterfly. In this strategy, we sell one in the money call option, Buy 2 at the money call options and sell one out of the money call option. This is a net credit strategy.

The maximum profit that one can receive by this strategy will be equal to the net credit received while initiating this strategy and the maximum loss will be the strike price of long call – the lower price – premiums received.

3. Long Put Butterfly

Long put butterfly is exactly similar to the long call butterfly options strategy but here you have to buy and sell put options instead of call options. In this strategy, the trader has to buy one in the money put option, short two at the money put options, and buy one out of the money put option. This is a net debit strategy.

Similar to long call butterfly this strategy will have a maximum profit when the underlying expires at the same price equal to the strike price of the short price. The maximum loss that can occur will be equal to the price of premiums paid initially.

4. Short Put Butterfly

Short put butterfly is similar exactly similar to the short Call butterfly but instead of call options, you have to sell and buy call options. In this strategy, the trader has to sell in the money call option, buy 2 at the money put options and sell out of the money put option.

The maximum profit that one can receive from this strategy will be equal to the net premiums received.

5. Iron Butterfly Strategy

The iron butterfly strategy is the combination of the long call butterfly and long put butterfly strategy. In this strategy, we buy one out of the money put option, one out of the money call option, and sell at the money call & put option.

The maximum profit will occur If the underlying stays range bound and expire at the middle strike price. The maximum loss in this strategy will be the price of long calls – the price of short calls – net premiums received.

This strategy is most suitable in order to capitalise on range-bound markets.

6. Reverse Iron Butterfly Strategy

This strategy is used when there is high volatility in the market. This strategy is exactly the opposite of the Iron Butterfly Strategy. In this strategy, we sell out of a money put option, one out of the money call option, and buy one at-the-money call & put option.

Option Buying Basics 1:- Choose The Correct Strike Price

Selection of the right strike price is an essential thing for the option buyer. Strike price matters a lot in option buying because even if you bet in the right direction and choose the wrong strike price, it will be of no use. When it comes to choosing the right strike price for option buying, there are two concepts that you need to understand.

The option is made up of two values, 1st is called intrinsic value, and 2nd part is called extrinsic value. The intrinsic value of the option is the value or points by which the option is in the money. Extrinsic value is nothing but the time value that is associated with that option. On the expiry day, the extrinsic value of the option becomes zero.

So, whenever you are trading in options, make sure that you are not buying deep out-of-the-money options because they have only extrinsic value, which will go to zero on the day of expiry, and there is more possibility that that particular option will expire worthless. Often, many new traders make this common mistake, and they lose a lot of money due to this.

Option Buying Basics 2:- Look At The Spot Chart

Which charts to look at..this is the most common question raised by new traders. New Options traders get confused about whether to refer to the spot chart or the options chart or the futures chart.

The answer to this question is simple. You need to refer to the spot chart, and according to the spot chart, you have to set your stop loss or target on the options chart. The reason behind preferring the spot chart is everything a trader needs to know is available on the spot chart, and futures and options charts follow the spot chart. Sometimes options charts may give you false information, but almost every time, the spot chart will show you the correct price action levels.

Option Buying Basics 3:- Don't Put All Your Capital In One Trade

Putting everything you got in one trade is a blunder. When trading options, you should only put 25 to 30% of your capital in one trade based on how good the opportunity market is offering to you.

Often, many traders put all of their capital in one trade, and when they book a loss, they end up losing a big percentage of money. By pre-defining the amount of capital deployed per trade, you can manage your risk very well. Also, you should pre-define your stop loss so that you can take the correct position sizing. When it comes to position sizing, you need to define your stop loss first, and then only you can take that trade.

Type Of Gaps In The Stock Market That Every Trader Should Know :

Gaps are an important topic to know about because, by understanding gaps, you can plan your trades. There are different types of gaps in the stock market, which are-

1. Common Gaps
2. Breakaway Gaps
3. Runaway Gaps
4. Exhaustion Gaps

When there is a greater difference between the bid and ask, gaps are created during those scenarios. Generally, most of the gaps are formed at the market opening because, in a live market, there is not much difference between the bid-ask spread and the current and that is why gaps are not created.

1. **Common Gaps**

As the name suggests, these are very small and common gaps. When the market opens sideways, and there is a very small gap between the price of today's open and yesterday's close, like -0.33% to +0.33%, then we can call it a common gap.

These gaps are filled quickly as compared to other gaps. Common gaps are also called "area gaps" or "trading gaps", and these gaps are represented by normal trading volume. These gaps generally do not offer any good trading opportunities

2. **Breakaway Gaps** : It is considered the strongest gap as compared to all other gaps. When the stock is consolidating, and when that consolidating range gets broken by the gap, then we can call it a Breakaway Gap. Generally, the Brakways gap indicates the starting of a new trend. The breakaway gap can be spotted in different types of chart patterns as well, such as ascending or descending triangle chart patterns, wedges etc.

3. **Runaway Gaps**

Run Away Gap represents the healthy trend. When there is no consolidation, but there is a gap between yesterday's closing and today's opening in the direction of the trend, then we call it Runaway Gap. The runway gap shows strength and can be used to book profits from existing swing positions. Generally, runaway gaps occur after the breakaway gaps, as the runway gap indicates the continuation of that particular trend. The runaway gap occurs in a strong bull or bear market.

4. Exhaustion Gap

As the name suggests exhaustion gap occurs at the end of the trend. Generally, the Exhaustion Gap is considered a trend reversal. Normally, the exhaustion gap is indicated when there is a big gap but the price reverses and fills that gap, and it continues that trend for a short-term period.

So, these are the 4 important types of Gaps every trader should know about. Every gap created in the market tries to indicate a potential move according to the gap theory; hence every trader must know what different types of gaps are and the significance of each gap.

Mistake avoid : Mistakes you should avoid to become a successful trader

Do you want to become a successful trader? Well, for that you have to avoid many common mistakes that traders often make. As you learn to trade you are going to make some mistakes, but your success depends upon how early you realize your mistake and find a way to overcome it. In this article, I am going to discuss the most common mistakes that traders make and also solutions to those mistakes to become a successful trader.

- **Starting to trade with real money instead of practicing to trade in a demo account.**

This is the worst possible mistake that a trader could ever make. But unfortunately, some amateur traders commit this mistake. In the beginning, traders are not familiar with the working of the account. As a result, they end up making errors such as not placing a stop loss properly or risking more money, etc. Thus, they end up damaging their account and eventually losing a lot of money. Hence, initially, you must practice trading in your demo account once you get familiar with all the things then you can trade with your real money.

Also, a demo account helps you to back test your strategy which is very important before using it in live markets. For becoming a successful trader your goal should be to back test every strategy on a demo trading account and your ability to trade it. So that you can trade with that strategy in live markets confidently.

- **Entering into multiple trades simultaneously and overtrading.**

This is the most common mistake that every amateur trader makes. About 90% of the traders end up on the losing side over the long-run when they are carrying out multiple trades simultaneously. Another interesting fact that you should know is if you have taken more than one trade at a time you are probably trading too much. It is illogical to be in more than one trade at any point of time if you are a beginner In trading.

Many amateur traders tend to overtrade because of many reasons like some traders want to recover their losses and some traders use trading systems without back-testing them. But the truth is unless you learn to control your emotions and stop over-trading, you are not going to be profitable in the long run.

Now if we talk about the solutions to these problems, the simplest solution is the realization of the fact that "you can make more money by taking less trades". By realizing this fact, you may begin to think that why a particular trade might not go in your favour instead of trying to find every single reason behind taking every trade.

- **Listening to news while trading**

Trading based on the news is the reason because of which many traders blow up their trading account. What happens is that traders go on the internet and start surfing the news related to trading or the financial world then they find some good or bad news about one particular stock and they try to trade that stock based on their opinions with heavy quantities and end up losing all the money. This happens because that news had already impacted the price of that particular stock before it came out.

Trading with price action techniques is always profitable rather than trading based on the news because news and other big events that affect the market is already reflected on the charts and by using price action you can easily identify it. In this way, you can actually trade the news and other big events without actually knowing them.

- **Not considering the worst-case scenario**

This error is related to trading psychology. Before taking any trade, you have to understand that every single trade you take has about equal chances of winning or losing irrespective of which strategy or which price action concept you use. It doesn't mean that you can't have a strategy which is having a higher percentage of win rate it simply means that for any given series of trades there can be a random outcome and the sequence of these outcomes depends upon many factors.

Now, let's say for example, you have a system which is having around 60% accuracy and out of the first 10 trades you lose 4 trades in a row but after these 4 losses, you could still win 60 percent of the time. If you don't maintain your calm during this losing streak and over-trade, you will surely be causing a lot of damage to your trading account. So, always have faith in your trading system and follow it properly.

A single trade simply does not mean anything. To analyse your ability to trade and how well your edge plays out, you need to learn to manage your risk over a large series of trades. Through this way, you can see if your trading system is profitable or not.

- **Feeling uncomfortable during trading and not following the trading plan.**

When you enter into the trade you should hold the trade unless your predetermined stop loss or target gets hit. You should not exit the trade in-between your target and stop-loss. Often many traders analyse the market and they find an opportunity in a particular stock then they enter into the trade and after some time they realise that the price has slightly moved against their favour and then they exit the trade immediately by fear. Here you have to understand that while trading you are going to have winning trades as well as losing trades but how much you lose in your losing trade and how much you win in your winning trade that matters the most. That's why you should follow your trading plan and you should not freak out when the market slightly moves against your favour.

- **Focusing on the profits and not the process**

When an amateur trader comes into the market, he wants to become a millionaire overnight. But it's the only impossible thing in this world. You have to understand that trading is not a trick which once you learned you will earn a lot of money through trading, rather than trading is a skill which takes time to develop and for developing a certain skill you should follow the process. Traders focus too much on the profits and reward but rather than focusing on the profits you should work on your trading system, trading psychology, and risk management. Remember, profit is the outcome of your process that's why always try to follow the process rather than focusing on profits.

- **Taking a late entry into the trade.**

It often happens with every trader; you analyse the market and you find a setup for entering into the trade but due to some reasons you didn't enter into that trade. And after some time when you see that price has already taken off from your imaginary entry point, then you get frustrated and rush to enter in a trade at a market price which is a big mistake. Instead of entering the trade, you have to pass that opportunity and remember; this is not the last opportunity there will be many opportunities yet to come.

• Not planning the stop loss and risk per trade before entering into the trade

Risk per trade is the maximum bearable loss that a trader can take on a single trade. Your risk per trade defines the quantity with which you should enter the particular trade.

Many new traders neglect these technical things and they enter into the trade with heavy quantities. If you are not managing the risk and blindly entering into the trades then it is high time for you to work on your risk management and capital preservation skills.

Key takeaways To Become a Successful Trader –

1. You are going to make mistakes as a trader but always learn from those mistakes.
2. You can earn more by trading less so stop over-trading
3. Always back-test your strategy before using it in a live market.
4. Never trade based on the news. Remember price action reflects everything on the charts.
5. Follow the process, not the profits.
6. Always pre-define your stop-loss and risk per trade.

Key Notes :

- **Success Chance 1% and 99% Probability of loss.**
- **Only Trade when you have proper knowledge and experience & Trend confirmation.**
- **Don’t Trade in no fluctuations or consolidation when no movement, no trend wait for one side trend**
- **Dont trend on expiry**
- **Dont trade with gap of out of money trade near the in the money or at the Money**
- **Dont take delivery or transfer next day**
- **Dont trade opposite of the market or trend**
- **Dont trade beacause you feel only trade when things are on chart**

- **Always use Action with defence technique or stop loss,set loss percentage which you can bear. no more than that, Dont overtrade**
- **Dont invest all your sallary, investment, loan, borrow, start with small.**

CHAPTER TEN

Strategies

There are many different strategies that traders can use in trading, and the right strategy for you will depend on your goals, risk tolerance, and trading style. Here are a few common trading strategies:

Day Trading: This strategy involves buying and selling securities within the same day, trying to profit from short-term price movements. Day traders often use technical analysis and chart patterns to identify potential trades.

Swing Trading: This strategy involves holding positions for several days or weeks, trying to profit from medium-term price movements. Swing traders often use a combination of technical analysis and fundamental analysis to identify potential trades.

Position Trading: This strategy involves holding positions for several months or even years, trying to profit from long-term price movements. Position traders often use fundamental analysis to identify undervalued securities with good growth prospects.

Trend Following: This strategy involves identifying trends in the market and then buying or selling securities that are likely to continue in the same direction. Trend followers often use technical indicators to identify trends and confirm price movements.

Contrarian Trading: This strategy involves going against the market consensus and taking positions that are opposite to the prevailing trend. Contrarian traders often use fundamental analysis to identify undervalued or overvalued securities.

These are just a few of the many trading strategies that traders use. It's important to remember that no strategy is foolproof, and successful trading requires a combination of skill, knowledge, and experience. It's also important to have a clear trading plan and to manage risk carefully to avoid losses.

Day Trading or Intraday :

Both day trading and intraday trading refer to a style of trading where a trader buys and sells securities within the same day. The terms are often used interchangeably, but there is a subtle difference between the two.

Day trading typically involves making multiple trades throughout the day in order to take advantage of small price movements in a stock, commodity, or currency. The aim is to close out all positions by the end of the trading day, and not carry any positions overnight. Day traders often use technical analysis to identify short-term trends and patterns in the market, and they may also use leverage to amplify their returns.

Intraday trading, on the other hand, may involve holding positions for a longer period of time during the day, perhaps for a few hours. Intraday traders also use technical analysis to identify trading opportunities, but they may focus more on medium-term trends rather than short-term fluctuations.

Overall, both day trading and intraday trading require a lot of skill, discipline, and risk management. They can be highly profitable if done correctly, but they also carry a significant amount of risk and are not suitable for everyone. It's important to have a solid understanding of the market, as well as a clear trading plan and risk management strategy, before engaging in either of these trading styles.

Essentials of Day Trading or Intraday :

Intraday or day trading is a type of trading where an investor buys and sells securities within the same trading day, with the goal of profiting from small price movements. This type of trading requires a specific set of skills and strategies to be successful, and some essential factors for intraday or day trading include:

Volatility: Intraday traders rely on price movements to make a profit, so they look for stocks or securities that have a high level of volatility. Stocks with low volatility may not offer enough price movement to generate significant profits.

Liquidity: Intraday traders need to be able to buy and sell stocks quickly, which requires high liquidity in the market. Stocks that have high trading volumes and tight bid-ask spreads are ideal for intraday trading.

Technical analysis: Intraday traders rely heavily on technical analysis to identify patterns and trends in the market. They use tools such as charts, indicators, and oscillators to help them make trading decisions.

Risk management: Intraday trading involves taking on a significant amount of risk, so it's essential to have a solid risk management strategy in place. Traders should be able to limit their losses and know when to exit a trade if it's not going in their favor.

Discipline and patience: Intraday trading requires a lot of discipline and patience, as traders need to be able to stick to their strategies and wait for the right opportunities to present themselves.

Overall, successful intraday or day trading requires a combination of skills, knowledge, and discipline, as well as a thorough understanding of the market and the securities being traded.

Trait a successful intaday trader :

Being a successful intraday trader requires a combination of knowledge, skills, and discipline. Here are some traits that can help an intraday trader achieve success:

Knowledge of the markets: A successful intraday trader has a deep understanding of the markets they trade in. This includes knowledge of market fundamentals, technical analysis, and market sentiment.

Discipline: Successful intraday traders are disciplined and stick to their trading plans. They do not deviate from their strategies based on emotions or outside influences.

Risk management: Intraday trading involves taking on significant risks, so successful traders must have a solid understanding of risk management. This includes setting stop-loss orders and limiting losses.

Technical skills: Intraday traders need to be proficient in using trading platforms and executing trades quickly. They also need to be able to analyze charts and technical indicators to make informed trading decisions.

Patience: Successful intraday traders are patient and wait for the right trading opportunities to present themselves. They do not rush into trades or make impulsive decisions.

Adaptability: Markets are constantly changing, and successful intraday traders must be able to adapt to these changes. They need to be flexible and adjust their trading strategies when market conditions change.

Emotional control: Intraday trading can be stressful, and successful traders need to be able to control their emotions. They do not let fear, greed, or other emotions influence their trading decisions.

Continuous learning: The markets are always evolving, so successful intraday traders need to be continuously learning and improving their trading strategies. They stay up to date with market news and trends, and they are always looking for ways to improve their trading performance.

Intraday Strategies :

- Select Quality stock over Quantity
- Stick to liquid Stock
- Find Stock with high volatility
- patience and consistency
- stick to the strategy
- Accuracy high
- No loan taken for trading Purpose
- If a trade goes wrong, book your losses and don't cling on to hope
- Choose Liquid Stocks
- Freeze the Exit and Entry Price
- Always Set a Stop Loss
- Book Profit When Target is Reached
- Always Close All your Positions
- Do not Challange the Market
- Research your Target Companies
- Good Entry Exit Timing
- Loss & Profit Booking
- Set Risk - Reward Ratio
-

Advantage and Disadvantage of Intraday Trading

Advantages of Intraday Trading:

Quick Profits: Intraday traders can make quick profits by taking advantage of short-term price movements in the market.

Lower Risk: Intraday trading involves lower risk as positions are closed before the end of the trading day, reducing the risk of overnight market movements.

High Liquidity: Intraday trading provides high liquidity as traders can buy and sell their positions quickly without affecting the market price.

Flexibility: Intraday traders have the flexibility to trade in different markets and securities.

Low Capital Requirement: Intraday trading requires lower capital as traders can use leverage to increase their buying power.

Disadvantages of Intraday Trading:

High Stress: Intraday trading can be stressful as traders need to constantly monitor the market and make quick decisions.

High Risk: Intraday trading involves high risk as prices can move against the trader, resulting in significant losses.

Overtrading: Intraday trading can lead to overtrading as traders may be tempted to take too many trades, resulting in lower profitability.

Market Volatility: Intraday trading is highly affected by market volatility, which can lead to unpredictable price movements.

Time-Consuming: Intraday trading requires a significant amount of time and dedication as traders need to be constantly monitoring the market and executing trades.

Overall, intraday trading can be a profitable venture for experienced traders who have a deep understanding of the markets and are willing to take on high risk.

Swing Trading :

Swing trading is a trading strategy that involves buying and selling financial assets, such as stocks, commodities, or currencies, with the aim of profiting from short-term price fluctuations. The basic idea of swing trading is to identify the up and down trends of an asset, and then buy or sell the asset when its price reaches certain levels.

Swing traders typically hold positions for a few days or weeks, rather than just a few hours or minutes, as is the case with day trading. The goal is to capture a portion of a price movement, and then exit the trade before the trend reverses.

Swing traders use a variety of technical analysis tools and charting techniques to identify entry and exit points for their trades. They also pay close attention to market news and other events that could affect the price of the asset they are trading.

Swing trading can be a profitable strategy for experienced traders who are able to manage their risk and have a solid understanding of technical analysis. However, it also involves a significant amount of risk, and traders should be prepared to suffer losses as well as make gains.

Essentials of Swing Trading :

Swing trading is a popular trading strategy that involves buying and selling securities within a short time frame, usually a few days to a few weeks, in order to profit from price movements. Here are some essentials of swing trading:

Identify stocks with potential: Swing traders typically look for stocks that have a strong price momentum or are showing signs of a potential trend reversal. Some traders also use technical analysis tools to identify entry and exit points for trades.

Set your entry and exit points: Once you have identified a stock to trade, you need to decide on your entry and exit points. This involves setting a target price for selling the stock at a profit and a stop-loss price to limit potential losses.

Manage risk: Swing trading can be risky, so it's important to manage risk. This can involve setting stop-loss orders to limit potential losses, diversifying your portfolio to spread risk, and being disciplined with your trading strategies.

Keep an eye on the market: Swing traders need to keep a close eye on the market and be prepared to act quickly when opportunities arise. This may involve monitoring news and events that could impact the market or specific stocks.

Develop a trading plan: To be successful in swing trading, it's important to have a well-defined trading plan. This should include your goals, trading strategies, risk management techniques, and an analysis of the market and stocks you plan to trade.

Practice discipline and patience: Swing trading requires discipline and patience. It's important to stick to your trading plan and not let emotions influence your trading decisions.

Overall, swing trading can be a lucrative strategy for traders who are willing to put in the time and effort to develop a sound trading plan, manage risk effectively, and be patient and disciplined in their trading.

Long Term Investment :

Long-term trading or investment refers to a strategy of holding an investment for an extended period of time, typically years or even decades, with the goal of realizing long-term gains.

The key difference between long-term trading and short-term trading or investing is the time horizon. Short-term traders seek to profit from short-term price movements in the market, whereas long-term traders or investors aim to capture the potential long-term growth of an investment.

Long-term trading or investing can be done in various assets such as stocks, bonds, real estate, mutual funds, and ETFs. It requires patience, discipline, and a strong belief in the fundamental strength of the investment. Long-term traders or investors typically make investment decisions based on factors such as the underlying company's financial health, growth prospects, and overall market trends.

Long-term trading or investing can also involve a buy-and-hold strategy, where investors hold onto an investment for a significant period of time, regardless of short-term market fluctuations. This approach is sometimes referred to as "passive investing" because it requires less frequent trading and less active management of one's portfolio.

Overall, long-term trading or investment can be a useful strategy for investors seeking to build wealth over time, but it requires careful planning, ongoing monitoring, and a commitment to the long-term outlook.

Essentials of Long Term Investment :

Long-term investment or trading is an approach to investing where an investor buys and holds assets for an extended period of time, typically for years or even decades. The goal of long-term investing is to build wealth gradually over time, taking advantage of the power of compound interest and the growth potential of the assets held. Here are some essentials of long-term investment or trading:

Develop a clear investment strategy: Before investing in any asset, it's essential to develop a clear investment strategy. This includes defining your investment objectives, risk tolerance, and time horizon. Your investment strategy should also consider the current economic environment, the performance of the asset class you are interested in, and any other relevant factors that could impact your returns.

Diversify your portfolio: Diversification is a critical component of long-term investing. By diversifying your portfolio, you can reduce your overall risk by spreading your investments across different asset classes and sectors. This helps to ensure that your portfolio is not overly exposed to any one particular investment, which can help to mitigate risk and minimize potential losses.

Focus on quality investments: When selecting investments for your portfolio, it's essential to focus on quality investments. This means investing in companies or assets that have a strong track record of performance, good management, and a sound financial position. Avoid investing in assets that are speculative or have a high degree of volatility, as these can lead to significant losses.

Monitor your investments: While long-term investing means holding assets for an extended period of time, it's still essential to monitor your investments regularly. This means keeping track of the performance of your investments and making adjustments as needed based on changes in the market or other relevant factors.

Stick to your investment plan: Finally, it's essential to stick to your investment plan over the long-term. This means avoiding the temptation to sell your investments during periods of market volatility or to chase after the latest hot investment trend. By staying disciplined and following your investment plan, you can help to ensure that you achieve your long-term investment goals.

Scalping in Trading : Scalping is a trading strategy used by traders to make quick profits by rapidly buying and selling financial instruments such as stocks, currencies, or commodities. The goal of scalping is to take advantage of small price movements and execute multiple trades in a short period of time, typically ranging from a few seconds to a few minutes.

Scalping requires traders to have a deep understanding of market conditions, price movements, and technical indicators. Traders who use this strategy often rely on technical analysis tools, such as charts and graphs, to identify potential entry and exit points for their trades.

Scalping can be a high-risk trading strategy, as traders must make quick decisions and execute trades with precision. It also requires a significant amount of focus and discipline, as traders need to be able to identify profitable trades quickly and act on them before market conditions change.

Overall, scalping can be an effective trading strategy for experienced traders who are willing to take on the risks associated with this approach. However, it is not recommended for inexperienced traders or those who are not comfortable with the high level of risk involved.

Averaging in Trading : Averaging or dollar-cost averaging, is a strategy used in trading and investing where a fixed amount of money is invested at regular intervals, regardless of the price of the asset being purchased. This is typically done to reduce the impact of market volatility on the overall performance of the investment.

For example, suppose an investor wants to invest $10,000 in a particular stock. Instead of investing the entire amount at once, they may choose to invest $1,000 per month for ten months. This way, if the price of the stock fluctuates over time, the investor will be buying at different price points, ultimately averaging out their cost.

Averaging can be a useful strategy for long-term investors who want to build a diversified portfolio over time. However, it is important to note that this strategy does not guarantee profits and may not be suitable for all investors or trading styles. Additionally, investors should always conduct thorough research and analysis before making any investment decisions.

Types of Trend ?

There are several types of trends that can be observed in the stock market.

Uptrend: This occurs when the market is experiencing a sustained increase in prices over time. It is characterized by a series of higher highs and higher lows.

Downtrend: This occurs when the market is experiencing a sustained decrease in prices over time. It is characterized by a series of lower highs and lower lows.

Sideways trend: This occurs when the market is trading within a range, with prices moving up and down within a relatively narrow band. consolidation no movement and low volatility.

Volatile trend: This occurs when the market experiences wide swings in prices over a short period of time.

Cyclical trend: This refers to the long-term trend in the market, which may be influenced by economic cycles or other macroeconomic factors.

Seasonal trend: This occurs when certain sectors or industries experience recurring patterns of activity based on seasonal factors, such as holidays or weather conditions.

It's important to note that trends can change over time, and no trend is guaranteed to continue indefinitely. Therefore, it is important for investors to stay informed about market conditions and adjust their investment strategies accordingly.

Key notes :

- **Look for reasonable profit**
- **Dont repeat the mistake, learn from your mistake and correct them.**
- **Leader of today may not be leader of tomorrow**
- **Set profit target, stop loss, technique trade in limit**
- **Always trade with market, Be creator or opportunist or trend with the flow of trend.**

CHAPTER ELEVEN

Risk Management

Risk management is an essential aspect of successful trading. It involves identifying, assessing, and controlling risks associated with financial markets' volatility and potential losses. Here are some key steps to effective risk management in trading:

- **Define your risk tolerance**: Before you start trading, it's important to determine the level of risk you're comfortable with. This will help you to set realistic goals and limit your exposure to potential losses.
- **Use stop-loss orders:** Stop-loss orders can help you limit your losses by automatically closing out a trade if the market moves against you beyond a certain point. This can help you avoid substantial losses.
- **Diversify your portfolio:** Diversifying your portfolio can help you spread your risk across multiple investments. This can help you mitigate the risk of significant losses.
- **Stay informed**: Keep up to date with the latest news and trends in the markets you're trading in. This can help you make informed decisions and avoid making hasty decisions based on emotions or incomplete information.
- **Monitor your trades:** It's important to regularly review and evaluate your trades to ensure you're sticking to your risk management plan. This can help you identify and address potential issues before they become significant problems.

Hedging :

Hedging is a risk management strategy used to reduce or offset the risks of adverse price movements in assets. It involves taking an offsetting position in a related asset or instrument that will provide a protective shield against potential losses.

Hedge funds are investment funds that use a range of sophisticated investment strategies to generate returns. The term "hedge fund" originally referred to a fund that used hedging strategies to mitigate the risks of investing in stocks or other assets. Today, however, hedge funds can use a variety of different investment strategies, and not all of them involve hedging.

Hedge funds often use leverage to amplify their returns, which also amplifies their risks. They typically have high minimum investments and are only available to accredited investors. Hedge funds are generally less regulated than other types of investment funds, which means that they have more freedom to pursue a wider range of investment strategies. However, this also means that they may be riskier than other types of investments.

Overall, while hedging is a specific risk management strategy, hedge funds are a type of investment fund that can use a range of strategies, including hedging, to generate returns.

here are various techniques that can be used to reduce losses and earn profits in the stock market. Here are some common strategies:

- **Diversification**: Diversification is the process of spreading your investments across different stocks, sectors, and asset classes. This strategy helps to reduce the risk of losses because if one stock or sector underperforms, the other holdings in the portfolio can help to offset the losses.
- **Fundamental analysis**: This strategy involves analyzing a company's financial statements, management, and other qualitative factors to determine its intrinsic value. By buying undervalued stocks, investors can potentially earn profits as the stock's true value is recognized by the market.
- **Technical analysis:** Technical analysis involves studying stock charts and market trends to identify patterns and make trading decisions. Traders who use this strategy try to predict future price movements based on past patterns.
- **Stop-loss orders**: A stop-loss order is an order to sell a stock when it reaches a certain price. This strategy is useful for limiting losses in case the stock price drops.
- **Rupees-cost averaging:** This strategy involves investing a fixed amount of money at regular intervals, regardless of the stock's price. This technique can help investors avoid the risk of investing a large amount of

money at the wrong time.

COMMON MISTAKE TO AVOID AS TRADER TO BE PROFITABLE

1. Not ready with a trading plan before trading.
2. Taking random trades.
3. Not having a loss plan.
4. Not putting right SL(stoploss).
5. Exist before Stop Loss.
6. Wrong position sizing.
7. Risk reward is less than or equal to 1:1.
8. Not holding winning trade and fear of missing out.
9. OVERTRADING.

THINGS TO DO FOR BECOMING PROFITABLE TRADERS

- Always plan your trade day before trading.
- Always write your trading journal.
- Always be ready with the right entry-level, target, and stop-loss.
- Always select a maximum of 5 stocks and trade maximum on 2 stocks only.
- Always avoid stocks in the news for Intraday.
- ALWAYS FOLLOW YOUR PLAN.

Beware from Stock Manupulation :

Stock manipulation refers to the intentional act of artificially influencing the price of a particular stock or securities in the financial market. This can be achieved through various methods, such as spreading false information, engaging in insider trading, or using other manipulative techniques to create an artificial demand for the stock.

Some common types of stock manipulation include:

Pump and dump schemes: This involves creating artificial demand for a stock by promoting it through false or misleading information. Once the price has risen, the manipulator will sell their shares, causing the price to plummet.

Insider trading: This involves using non-public information to make trades that benefit the trader or their associates, often at the expense of other investors.

Spoofing: This involves placing fake orders to create the illusion of demand or supply, and then cancelling the orders once the market reacts to the fake data.

Invest in what you know :

The advice to "invest in what you know" is a common piece of wisdom given to investors, and it essentially means that you should invest in companies or industries that you understand and have knowledge about. The idea behind this advice is that if you have a good understanding of a company or industry, you're more likely to make sound investment decisions and avoid costly mistakes.

Here are a few reasons why investing in what you know can be a good idea:

You can better evaluate potential investments: If you understand an industry or company, you're more likely to be able to evaluate its potential for growth, profitability, and other important factors. You can also more easily identify risks and potential problems.

You can avoid "hot tips" and fads: Sometimes people are tempted to invest in the latest hot stock or trend, even if they don't understand the company or industry. By focusing on what you know, you can avoid this temptation and stick to investments that you have a good understanding of.

You can stay informed: If you invest in what you know, you'll likely already be following news and developments in the industry or company. This can help you make informed decisions and stay up-to-date on any changes that could impact your investments.

However, it's important to note that investing in what you know isn't foolproof. You still need to do your due diligence and research before making any investment decisions, even if you're familiar with the company or industry. It's also important to diversify your portfolio to spread out risk and avoid over-investing in any one area.

The sell condition of a stock refers to the criteria or factors that an investor or trader uses to decide when to sell their shares of a particular stock. These conditions can vary depending on an individual's investment strategy, risk tolerance, and financial goals.

Some common sell conditions for stocks include:

Target price: An investor may set a specific price at which they will sell their shares of a stock. This target price may be based on the investor's assessment of the stock's fair value or expected future performance.

Stop-loss order: A stop-loss order is a type of order that instructs a broker to sell a stock if its price falls below a certain level. This can help limit potential losses in the event that the stock's price declines rapidly.

Technical analysis: Some traders use technical analysis to identify trends or patterns in a stock's price chart. They may use indicators such as moving averages, support and resistance levels, or momentum indicators to determine when to sell their shares.

Fundamental analysis: Investors may use fundamental analysis to assess a company's financial health and growth potential. They may sell their shares if they believe the company's fundamentals have deteriorated or if the stock's valuation has become too high relative to its earnings or other financial metrics.

Diversification: Finally, some investors may sell shares of a stock simply to rebalance their portfolio or reduce their exposure to a particular sector or industry. This can help manage risk and ensure that their portfolio is well-diversified.

The buy condition of a stock refers to the criteria or factors that an investor considers before deciding to purchase shares of a particular company. These conditions typically vary depending on the investor's personal investment strategy, risk tolerance, and financial goals. Some common factors that investors might consider when evaluating a stock's buy condition include:

Valuation: Investors may look at the stock's price-to-earnings (P/E) ratio, price-to-book (P/B) ratio, or other valuation metrics to determine if the stock is undervalued or overvalued.

Fundamentals: Investors may evaluate a company's financial performance, including revenue growth, earnings growth, profit margins, and debt levels, to determine if it is a sound investment.

Industry trends: Investors may consider the trends and outlook for the industry in which the company operates, as well as any potential disruptors or competitors that could impact the company's future performance.

Management: Investors may evaluate the quality and experience of the company's management team, as well as their track record of making sound strategic decisions.

Macro factors: Investors may consider broader economic factors, such as interest rates, inflation, and geopolitical risks, that could impact the company's performance.

Overall, the buy condition of a stock will depend on a variety of factors, and investors should conduct thorough research and analysis before making any investment decisions.

The buy condition of a stock refers to the criteria or factors that an investor considers before deciding to purchase shares of a particular company. These conditions typically vary depending on the investor's personal investment strategy, risk tolerance, and financial goals. Some common factors that investors might consider when evaluating a stock's buy condition include:

Valuation: Investors may look at the stock's price-to-earnings (P/E) ratio, price-to-book (P/B) ratio, or other valuation metrics to determine if the stock is undervalued or overvalued.

Fundamentals: Investors may evaluate a company's financial performance, including revenue growth, earnings growth, profit margins, and debt levels, to determine if it is a sound investment.

Industry trends: Investors may consider the trends and outlook for the industry in which the company operates, as well as any potential disruptors or competitors that could impact the company's future performance.

Management: Investors may evaluate the quality and experience of the company's management team, as well as their track record of making sound strategic decisions.

Macro factors: Investors may consider broader economic factors, such as interest rates, inflation, and geopolitical risks, that could impact the company's performance.

Overall, the buy condition of a stock will depend on a variety of factors, and investors should conduct thorough research and analysis before making any investment decisions.

How to implement risk management in trading?

- **Do not take the trade without planning a stop loss**

Taking the trade without setting the stop loss is like driving the break failed vehicle on the highway. You will never know when there will be an accident. As a trader capital preservation must be your first goal then you can think about growing up your trading account. Remember, "rules of engagement 101 for trading": NEVER leave your bank account unprotected when you go out to fight the "battle" of trading. Now the question remains, what does that mean to you as a trader and the most important question is how to apply it?

It means that you should not trade with your real money unless you have your detailed trading plan. Your trading plan must include various things like a maximum loss that you can bear, what is your risk per trade? Which signals can be taken as confirmation before entering into the trade? Of course, there are many more things which should be considered but these are the most important things among all.

- **Why is capital preservation important?**

Usage of excessive leverage is considered a big risk in trading and it is the main reason behind the blowouts of trading accounts. Even the best traders can lose all their money due to excessive leverage.

Here the point we should understand is there are many good traders in the world some of them even get employed by major trading firms. However, not all of them can generate significant returns from trading because they fail in managing the risk of capital and capital preservation.

A "good trader" Is not just someone who can analyze the charts and predict the next move of the market, but someone who can manage the risk of their capital with steady returns and can do this consistently with a trading edge. If you are lacking in your capital preservation skills then someday you will be ending up on the losing side. For long-term success in trading, you should practice capital preservation again and again.

The Process to be followed for making money as a trader-

Limit all your losses up to the certain level which you are comfortable with losing on any trade.

Try to develop a trading edge so that you will have bigger profits combined with smaller losses.

Don't try complicated things, remember only simple things work in the market.

Risk to Reward ratio- it is the ratio of the total risk of your capital to potential reward on a single trade. If the risk-reward ratio is less than one then it doesn't make any sense. Look for the trade which is having a risk-reward ratio greater than one. If you are getting a trade which is having a risk-reward ratio of less than one then leave that opportunity and wait for another one.

Setting up the stop-loss- stop-loss placement is the key factor while planning your trade because it determines your position sizing and position sizing is nothing but how you control your risk.

Position sizing- position sizing is nothing but determining how many lots or contracts you are trading during a single trade. It's the distance between the stop-loss and entry point combined with the position size that decides the amount of money you are risking on a trade.

Setting up the targets- You have to set the target levels logically. There are multiple ways by which you can place your targets like previous support and resistance, and daily market range, etc.

Psychology of the trader while exiting the trade-Do not get emotionally attached with your positions, cut your losses at predetermined levels, and follow your trading plan.

Key Notes :

- **Do not take a trade without planning.**
- **More than your trading system and trading psychology risk management is important.**
- **Make sure to make capital preservation your primary goal while trading.**
- **Always follow your trading plan and develop a trading edge.**
- **Trade only active stocks which are volatile**
- **Bear markets have no support and Bull markets have no resistance**

CHAPTER TWELVE

Goal in Financial Market

The goal in financial market can vary depending on individual's financial situation, risk appetite, and investment strategy. However, in general, the primary goal in financial market is to earn a return on invested capital or assets. This can be achieved through various investment instruments, such as stocks, bonds, mutual funds, exchange-traded funds (ETFs), real estate, and commodities.

Investors may have short-term or long-term goals. Short-term goals may include generating income or achieving quick gains through trading strategies. Long-term goals may include building wealth for retirement, funding children's education, or leaving a legacy for future generations.

In addition to earning a return on investment, investors may also aim to minimize risk and preserve capital. This can be accomplished through diversification, asset allocation, and risk management strategies.

Overall, the goal in financial market is to make informed investment decisions that align with one's financial goals, risk tolerance, and time horizon, and ultimately help achieve long-term financial success.

Short-term and long-term goals in the stock market can vary depending on individual investment objectives and risk tolerance.

Short-term goals in the stock market typically involve investments with a duration of less than a year. These goals may include generating quick profits or taking advantage of short-term market fluctuations. Examples of short-term investment strategies may include day trading, swing trading, or investing in stocks that are expected to perform well in the short term.

Long-term goals in the stock market typically involve investments with a duration of several years or more. These goals may include generating wealth through capital appreciation, dividend income, or a combination of both. Examples of long-term investment strategies may include investing in blue-chip stocks, exchange-traded funds (ETFs), or mutual funds that are diversified across different sectors.

It is important to note that short-term goals in the stock market are generally riskier than long-term goals, as short-term investments are often subject to market volatility and can be influenced by a variety of factors. On the other hand, long-term investments may offer more stability and the potential for greater returns over time. Ultimately, the best approach to investing in the stock market will depend on an individual's financial goals, risk tolerance, and investment timeframe.

One Day Goal : The goal of intraday trading is to buy and sell securities within the same trading day, taking advantage of small price movements to generate profits. Intraday traders typically focus on short-term price fluctuations and use technical analysis tools to identify opportunities to enter and exit positions.

The primary objective of intraday trading is to generate profits by taking advantage of small price movements. To achieve this, intraday traders use various trading strategies, including scalping, news trading, and trend following. However, intraday trading can be risky, and it requires discipline, patience, and a good understanding of the market and trading tools.

Some common goals of intraday traders include making a certain percentage return on their capital, achieving a specific number of profitable trades, or sticking to a specific trading plan or strategy. Ultimately, the goal of intraday trading is to make consistent profits over time by successfully executing trades based on a well-defined trading plan and risk management strategy.

Key notes :

- **The smarter you are the longer it takes**
- **Control what you can , manage what you can not**
- **Big movemrnt take time to develop**
- **A good trade is profitabe right from the start**
- **Avoid partnership in trading account**
- **Dont trade in emotion trade in practical**
- **Expert in one thing other than maney more**

CHAPTER THIRTEEN

Investment

Investing refers to the act of committing money or capital to an endeavor with the expectation of obtaining an additional income or profit in the future. There are many ways to invest, including but not limited to stocks, bonds, real estate, mutual funds, and commodities.

Here are some basic steps on how to invest:

Set investment goals: Before investing, it's essential to identify your goals and investment objectives, such as saving for retirement, purchasing a home, or growing your wealth.

Create a budget: A budget can help you determine how much you can afford to invest regularly and over a longer-term.

Educate yourself: Investing requires some level of knowledge and understanding of financial markets, investment vehicles, and risks associated with them. So it's essential to do some research, read books, attend seminars or seek advice from experts.

Choose your investment options: Once you have identified your goals and understand the risks, you can begin to consider different investment options that align with your goals, risk tolerance, and financial resources.

Monitor and adjust your portfolio: Regular monitoring of your investments is essential to ensure that they continue to align with your investment goals and risk tolerance. Sometimes you may need to adjust your portfolio based on market conditions, your financial situation or changing goals.

What Is Value Investing?

Value investing is an investment strategy that involves picking stocks that appear to be trading for less than their intrinsic or book value. Value investors actively ferret out stocks they think the stock market is underestimating. They believe the market overreacts to good and bad news, resulting in stock price movements that do not correspond to a company's long-term fundamentals. The overreaction offers an opportunity to profit by buying stocks at discounted prices—on sale.

The basic concept behind everyday value investing is straightforward: If you know the true value of something, you can save a lot of money when you buy it on sale. Most folks would agree that whether you buy a new TV on sale, or at full price, you're getting the same TV with the same screen size and picture quality.

Value investors actively ferret out stocks they think the stock market is underestimating.

Value investors use financial analysis, don't follow the herd, and are long-term investors of quality companies.

Value investing is the process of doing detective work to find these secret sales on stocks and buying them at a discount compared to how the market values them. In return for buying and holding these value stocks for the long term, investors can be rewarded handsomely.

Margin of Safety :

Value investors require some room for error in their estimation of value, and they often set their own "margin of safety," based on their particular risk tolerance. The margin of safety principle, one of the keys to successful value investing, is based on the premise that buying stocks at bargain prices gives you a better chance at earning a profit later when you sell them. The margin of safety also makes you less likely to lose money if the stock doesn't perform as you had expected.

Value investors use the same sort of reasoning. If a stock is worth $100 and you buy it for $66, you'll make a profit of $34 simply by waiting for the stock's price to rise to the $100 true value. On top of that, the company might grow and become more valuable, giving you a chance to make even more money. If the stock's price rises to $110, you'll make $44 since you bought the stock on sale. If you had purchased it at its full price of $100, you would only make a $10 profit.

Markets Are Not Efficient :

Value investors don't believe in the efficient-market hypothesis, which says that stock prices already take all information about a company into account, so their price always reflects their value. Instead, value investors believe that stocks may be over- or underpriced for a variety of reasons.

For example, a stock might be underpriced because the economy is performing poorly and investors are panicking and selling (as was the case during the Great Recession). Or a stock might be overpriced because investors have gotten too excited about an unproven new technology (as was the case of the dot-com bubble). Psychological biases can push a stock price up or down based on news, such as disappointing or unexpected earnings announcements, product recalls, or litigation. Stocks may also be undervalued because they trade under the radar, meaning they're inadequately covered by analysts and the media.

Don't Follow the Herd :

Value investors possess many characteristics of contrarians—they don't follow the herd. Not only do they reject the efficient-market hypothesis, but when everyone else is buying, they're often selling or standing back. When everyone else is selling, they're buying or holding. Value investors don't buy trendy stocks (because they're typically overpriced). Instead, they invest in companies that aren't household names if the financials check out. They also take a second look at stocks that are household names when those stocks' prices have plummeted, believing such companies can recover from setbacks if their fundamentals remain strong and their products and services still have quality

Know What Kind of Investor You Are

Active vs. Passive Investors - Day trder and Long term Investor

Speculator vs. Investor - Future option or Day trading and Investiment in quality stocks.

World Top Investors :

1. Benjamin Graham
2. Warren Buffet
3. John Templeton
4. Jim Simons
5. Thomas Rowe Price Jr.
6. Peter Lynch
7. George Soros
8. Jesse Livermore
9. John Neff
10. William H. Gross
11. Philip Fisher
12. Carl Icahn

Jesse Livermore- Jesse Livermore was a legendary trader and investor who made a fortune in the stock market during the early 20th century. His strategies and principles of investment are still relevant today, and many investors continue to study his methods in order to improve their own trading and investing.

Here are some of the key strategies and principles that Jesse Livermore used:

Follow the trend: Livermore believed that the market is always right and that the key to success is to follow the trend. He would only take positions in the direction of the trend and avoid trading against it.

Cut losses quickly: Livermore was a firm believer in cutting losses quickly. He would never hold onto a losing position for too long and would cut his losses as soon as he realized that he was wrong.

Let profits run: On the other hand, Livermore would let his winning trades run as far as they could go. He believed that if a trade was going in his favor, there was no reason to exit the position prematurely.

Use stop-loss orders: Livermore was one of the first traders to use stop-loss orders to protect his positions. He would set a stop-loss order at a predetermined price level to limit his losses in case the trade went against him.

Be patient: Livermore was known for his patience and discipline. He would wait for the right opportunity to present itself before entering a trade, and he would never chase after the market or try to force trades.

Stay humble: Livermore understood the importance of staying humble and not getting too attached to his positions. He would always be willing to admit when he was wrong and cut his losses, even if it meant taking a hit to his ego.

Study the market: Finally, Livermore was a firm believer in studying the market and understanding the underlying factors that drove it. He would spend hours studying market trends and analyzing data in order to make informed investment decisions.

Warren Buffett :Warren Buffettis one of the most successful investors of all time, and his investment strategies and principles have been studied and emulated by investors around the world. Here are some of the key strategies and principles that Warren Buffett has used:

Invest in what you understand: Buffett believes in investing in companies and industries that he understands well. He has a preference for businesses with simple, easy-to-understand models and avoids those with complex or opaque structures.

Value investing: Buffett is known as a value investor, which means he looks for companies that are undervalued by the market but have strong fundamentals, such as a good track record, strong management, and a competitive advantage.

Long-term focus: Buffett is a long-term investor and believes in holding onto stocks for the long haul. He has said that his favorite holding period is "forever" and that he looks for companies that have a sustainable competitive advantage and can continue to grow over the long term.

Patience and discipline: Buffett is known for his patience and discipline when it comes to investing. He doesn't make impulsive decisions and is willing to wait for the right opportunity to come along.

Margin of safety: Buffett believes in the concept of a margin of safety, which means buying stocks at a price that provides a cushion against potential downside risks. This helps to reduce the risk of losing money on investments.

Avoid market timing: Buffett doesn't believe in trying to time the market or make short-term bets on stocks. Instead, he focuses on buying quality companies at a good price and holding onto them for the long term.

Continuous learning: Buffett is a voracious reader and believes in the importance of continuous learning. He spends a lot of time reading and studying companies and industries in order to make informed investment decisions.

Dow Theory : Dow Theory is a set of principles and strategies developed by Charles Dow, the founder of the Dow Jones & Company, in the late 19th and early 20th centuries. These principles were the basis of the technical analysis of the stock market and have become an important part of modern investment theory.

The Dow Theory is based on six principles that help investors determine the long-term trend of the stock market. These principles include:

The market discounts everything: The stock market reflects all information available, including political, economic, and financial factors.

There are three trends in the stock market: The stock market has three trends – the primary trend (long-term trend), the secondary trend (medium-term trend), and the minor trend (short-term trend).

The primary trend is the most important: The primary trend is the most important and can last from one to several years. The secondary and minor trends are corrective movements within the primary trend.

The trend is confirmed by volume: The trend is confirmed by increasing volume during an uptrend and decreasing volume during a downtrend.

The trend remains in effect until a clear reversal occurs: The trend remains in effect until a clear reversal occurs, which is signaled by a change in the primary trend.

The averages must confirm each other: The Dow Jones Industrial Average and the Dow Jones Transportation Average should move in the same direction to confirm a trend.

Benjamin Graham : Benjamin Graham was a prominent economist and investor who is widely considered to be the father of value investing. He is best known for his influential books on investing, including "The Intelligent Investor" and "Security Analysis."

The Benjamin Graham strategy is a value investing approach that involves looking for undervalued companies with strong financials and a track record of stable earnings growth. This strategy involves a deep analysis of a company's financial statements, looking at factors such as its price-to-earnings ratio, dividend yield, and debt-to-equity ratio. The goal is to find companies that are trading at a discount to their intrinsic value, which can be determined through a careful analysis of the company's financials.

The principle of investment according to Benjamin Graham is to buy stocks that are undervalued, and to hold them for the long term. This approach is based on the idea that the stock market can be irrational in the short term, but over the long term, the market will eventually recognize the true value of a company. By buying undervalued stocks and holding onto them for the long term, investors can benefit from the market's eventual correction and earn strong returns.

Graham also emphasized the importance of diversification in investing. He believed that investors should spread their investments across a range of different stocks, bonds, and other assets to reduce the risk of loss. This approach can help investors to weather market downturns and avoid the risks associated with investing in a single company or sector.

Overall, the Benjamin Graham strategy and principles of investment emphasize the importance of careful analysis, patience, and diversification in achieving long-term investment success.

Cyclical investing : Cyclical investing is an investment strategy that involves buying stocks or other assets that are expected to perform well during certain phases of the economic cycle. Cyclical stocks are those that are particularly sensitive to changes in the economy, and tend to perform well when the economy is growing and expanding, but may struggle when the economy is contracting.

Examples of cyclical stocks include companies in industries such as retail, automotive, construction, and travel and leisure. During periods of economic growth, these companies tend to see increased demand for their products and services, leading to higher profits and stock prices. However, during economic downturns, these companies may struggle as demand for their products and services decreases.

Investors who practice cyclical investing often try to time the market by buying cyclical stocks during economic expansions and selling them before economic contractions. This can be a risky strategy, as predicting economic cycles is difficult, and cyclical stocks can be volatile and unpredictable.

Overall, cyclical investing can be a way for investors to potentially earn higher returns during periods of economic growth, but it requires careful research and analysis to identify the right stocks and timing for buying and selling them.

sector rotation

Sector rotation is an investment strategy that involves shifting investments from one industry or sector to another in response to changing economic conditions and market trends. This strategy aims to take advantage of the cyclical nature of different sectors, as well as their varying performances in different stages of the economic cycle.

For example, during a period of economic expansion, cyclical sectors such as technology, consumer discretionary, and industrials may outperform defensive sectors such as healthcare, utilities, and consumer staples. Conversely, during a recession or market downturn, defensive sectors may provide more stability and resilience compared to cyclical sectors.

Investors who employ sector rotation strategy typically use a top-down approach, where they analyze macroeconomic indicators and market trends to identify which sectors are likely to perform well in the current market environment. They then allocate their investments accordingly, either by buying individual stocks or exchange-traded funds (ETFs) that track specific sectors.

It is worth noting that sector rotation is a form of active investing, and as such, it carries higher risks and requires more skill and research compared to passive investing strategies such as index investing. Additionally, there is no guarantee that any particular sector will outperform or underperform in any given period, so investors must carefully assess their risk tolerance and investment objectives before implementing this strategy.

the trading plan that you should follow before you make a trade on the stock. Also, we will be talking about the many Do's and Don'ts that are mostly missed by the traders, as a result, they lose their money in the market. Please do follow these points and include them in your trading plan to make yourself a better trader.

1.S (Stock or Script): – You should know which stock are you going to trade on.

A. R (Reason): – What is the reason for trading on this stock? There can be many reasons, some of them are as follows

Any crossover given by EMA or MACD depending on the movement of the stock

Volume or ADX is increasing

RSI is giving a breakout

Basically, any reason that comes up for trading on a stock.

1. P (Plan): – Always know which strategy you are using and make sure you are following all the rules of that strategy.

3. S (Stop Loss and Target): – Always choose Logical Stop loss and target.

    a. For Stop-loss, find logical support or resistance like any EMA or pivot level or any previous level and keep the stop loss just a little below it.

    b. For Target find a logical support or resistance level where you feel the price will not go above or below that level.

4. Q (Quantity): – Always know how much quantity you have to trade for according to your capital and your appetite for a Loss. Never go in for a larger quantity if you have any fear or doubt in that trade.

5. T (Time): – Always know for how much time you are going to hold that stock based on your target. For example

30 Minutes

1 Hour

3 hours

Till the end of the day(Intraday)
Two days(BTST)
More than two days

DO'S AND DON'T'S

Do's

1. Always keep yourself updated on all the latest movements and news (But don't trade on news)

2. Do homework every day

Look at least 4-5 charts from the watchlist.
Check past support and resistance near the current price level.
Check volume, ADX, and RSI levels on those stocks.

3. Think in terms of percentage, not in terms of money.

4. Follow "SRPSQT"

5. Keep your trade book near you while trading.

6. Keep a regular check all the time frames for intraday (5M, 15M,30M).

7. Think small in Intraday. If you intend to think big then think systematically, have patience. Patience is the key when you're thinking big.

8. Keep your targets in mind.

9. Keep writing your daily plans.

10. Read books every day

11. Have patience as per your "T" in SRPSQT.

12. Buy at support. At reversal from the bottom

13. Sell at resistance. At reversal from the top.

14. Always do the closing and write your journal every day.
15. Alway Remember why you started Trading.

Don't's

1. Never trade on stocks with low or FallingADX.
2. No entry without"SRPSQT".
3. Do not enter with less energy.
4. Don't ignore the END GOAL (DailyTarget).
5. If you fear, Exit from the trade or half the quantity.
6. Never regret on a missed opportunity, it creates rush which results in the wrong trade.
7. Don't think big in Intraday, Only in the longterm.
8. Don't travel and trade. If you still want to, do it for a smaller quantity.
9. Don't take more than two trades in a day (Go for the third only if it's a 5STAR OPPORTUNITY)
10. Never do REVENGE TRADE.
11. Never be Arrogant while trading and after trading.
12. Remove FOMO (FEAR OF MISSING OUT).
13. Never have EGO. Getting wrong trades? Take a break, do with less quantity
14. Don't focus on profits. Focus on the PROCESS.
15. Never do SCALPING (Random buying and selling looking at small moves)
16. If doing BTST, do it only for a lesser quantity. Especially for options.
17. Never trade by watching the news.

Key note :

- **Money Can not be made evey day in the market, you cant perfect always**
- **Follow your rules**
- **Research, Analyse,Select, Practice and achive the target**
- **Dont be overconfidence, keep patience Balance and seek and use opportunist**
- **Invest in Different sector Mutual fund, fd ,currency, commodity, avoid future option**
- **Never depend on single or invest in one place.**

CHAPTER FOURTEEN

Questions & Answers Related Stock

1. **What is a stock?** A stock, also known as a share or equity, is a unit of ownership in a company. When you buy a stock, you become a shareholder in that company, which gives you the right to a portion of the company's profits and assets.
2. **How do I buy stocks?** You can buy stocks through a brokerage account, which you can open with an online broker or a traditional broker. Once you have a brokerage account, you can place orders to buy and sell stocks through the broker's platform.
3. **What is the stock market?** The stock market refers to the collection of exchanges and markets where stocks and other securities are bought and sold. Some of the largest stock markets in the world include the New York Stock Exchange (NYSE), NASDAQ, and the Tokyo Stock Exchange.
4. **What is a stock index?** A stock index is a measurement of the performance of a group of stocks that are representative of a specific market or sector. Examples of popular stock indices include the S&P 500, the Dow Jones Industrial Average, and the NASDAQ Composite.
5. **What is a dividend?** A dividend is a distribution of a portion of a company's earnings to its shareholders. Companies can choose to pay out dividends to shareholders as a way to return value to them.
6. **What is a stock split?** A stock split is a corporate action where a company increases the number of its outstanding shares by issuing more shares to its existing shareholders. The goal of a stock split is to make the shares more affordable to a wider range of investors.
7. **What is a stock option?** A stock option is a contract that gives an investor the right to buy or sell a stock at a certain price within a certain

time frame. Stock options are often used by investors as a way to hedge risk or speculate on the price movements of a stock.

8. **What is insider trading?** Insider trading is the act of buying or selling a stock based on material, non-public information about a company that is not available to the general public. Insider trading is illegal and can result in significant fines and jail time.
9. **What is a bear market?** A bear market is a term used to describe a prolonged period of declining stock prices, typically defined as a decline of 20% or more from recent highs. Bear markets can be caused by a variety of factors, including economic downturns, political uncertainty, or changes in investor sentiment.
10. **What is a bull market?** A bull market is a term used to describe a prolonged period of rising stock prices. Bull markets are typically characterized by strong economic growth, low unemployment, and investor optimism.
11. **What is limit order ?** To avoid buying or selling a stock at a price higher or lower than you wanted, you need to place a limit order rather than a market order. A limit order is an order to buy or sell a security at a specific price. You could use a limit order when you want to set the price of the stock. In other words, you want to sell/buy particular scrip at a price other than the current market price. However, although a limit order guarantees a price, it cannot guarantee execution of the trade. This is because the stock might not reach the desired price on that particular trading day owing to market-related factors.
12. **What is stop Loss order** ? A stop loss order is a normal order placed with a broker to sell a security when it reaches a certain predetermined price called the trigger price. Sometimes the market movements defy your expectations. Such market reversals often result in loss-bearing transactions. The stop loss trigger price is your defense mechanism – an amount at which you will be able to sustain yourself against such unanticipated market movements. For example, if you bought a stock at Rs. 10, you place a stop loss order with your broker to sell it, if it reaches Rs. 8. This helps you prevent further loss, in the eventuality that the price of the stock might dip even further. Thus, it helps limit your loss or protect unrealized profits, whichever the case.
13. **What is Day order** ? GTC or Day Orders are orders given to your broker that hold true only during the trading day when the order was placed. If the order has not been executed on that day, it will not be passed on

to the next trading day. Thus, they are orders that are only 'good until it is canceled' or 'good for the day'. For example, suppose that you have placed a stop loss order with your broker to sell a stock once the price reaches level X. If it does not reach limit X, your broker will not sell the stock. However, the stop loss order given to your broker will not hold true for the next day. So, even if the stock reaches level X on Day 2, he will not execute the trade till you instruct him to do so again.

14. **What is a Broker** ? Brokers—also known as trading members—perform a vital function in the stock market. They execute transactions such as the buying and selling of stocks on behalf of their clients. In return for this, they charge a brokerage commission.
15. **Why Stock Price Fluctuate** ? Once shares enter the secondary market, their prices are governed by the laws of supply and demand. Let's consider three basic scenarios: Besides, several other things affect the demand and supply of stocks, and thereby influence the stock prices. Here are some common factors that investors should note: **Company performance**: If the company's earnings have exceeded expectations, demand for the company's shares is sure to rise. This will lead the stock price to increase. But if there is a decline in the company's performance, more stockholders may wish to sell their shares in a market where buyers are few. In such a situation, the stock price could fall. **Sector performance:** You will find that the stock prices of companies in the same sector tend to move in a similar way. If the entire sector is seeing bullish trends, stock prices of companies within the sector are likely to rise. But if the mood is bearish, the stock prices could fall. **News events**: Economic announcements like a change in the repo rate could affect the cost of debt for a company. This could affect its stock prices. Political events like a change in the governance of a country could also affect stock price movements.
16. **What is Equities and Derivaties** ? **The equity market** deals with the stocks of the companies. When you buy a company's stock, you gain part-ownership of the company. **The derivatives** markets deals in futures and options (F&O). These are financial contracts that derive their value from certain underlying assets, such as shares, commodities, and currencies. In the stock derivatives market, the underlying assets are equities
17. **Stock Vs Share** ? 'Stock' represents the holder's part-ownership in one or several companies. Meanwhile, 'share' refers to a single unit of

ownership in a company.

18. What is FII & Dii ?

    FII and DII are two terms commonly used in the Indian stock market to refer to different types of investors.

    FII stands for Foreign Institutional Investor, which refers to institutional investors based outside of India who invest in Indian financial markets. These include hedge funds, mutual funds, pension funds, and other institutional investors who invest in India's stock market and debt market.

    DII stands for Domestic Institutional Investor, which refers to institutional investors based in India who invest in Indian financial markets. These include mutual funds, insurance companies, banks, and other financial institutions that invest in India's stock market and debt market.

19. **what is volatility?** Volatility of a stock refers to the degree of variation in the price of a stock over time. It is a statistical measure of the dispersion of returns for a given security or market index. In simple terms, it is the degree of fluctuation in the price of a stock in a given period of time.
20. **What is vix** ? VIX (CBOE Volatility Index) is a widely used financial metric that measures the expected volatility of the stock market over the next 30 days. It is often referred to as the "fear index" because it tends to rise during times of market uncertainty, instability, or panic.
21. **What is Penny stock** ? Penny stocks are those that trade at a very low price, have very low market capitalisation, are mostly illiquid, and are usually listed on a smaller exchange.
22. **Small Cap Companies** ? Small-cap companies are those that have a market capitalisation of less than Rs 5,000 crore. These companies are relatively smaller in size and have significant growth potential. What makes them risky is the low probability that they will be successful over time. This makes the stocks of such companies volatile in nature. Small-cap companies have a long history of underperformance but when an economy is emerging out of a recession, small-cap stocks often prove to be outperformers.
23. **Mid Cap Companies** ? Mid-cap companies are companies whose market cap is above Rs 5,000 crore but less than Rs 20,000 crore. Investing in these companies can be riskier than investing in large-cap market companies. This is because mid-caps tend to be more volatile. On the other hand, mid-cap companies also have the ability to turn into large-

cap companies in the long run

24. **Bluechip or Large Cap Companies?** Large-cap companies are businesses that are well-established and have a significant market share. Large-cap companies have market caps of Rs 20,000 crore or more. These companies dominate the industry and are very stable. They hold themselves well in times of recession or during any other negative event. Besides, they will usually have been functioning for decades and have good reputations. If you want to invest in a company's stocks by taking less risk, then large-cap stocks are a good option. These stocks are less volatile in comparison to mid-cap and small-cap stocks. The lower volatility makes them less risky.
25. **Short Selling** ? Short selling occurs when an investor borrows a security and sells it on the open market, planning to buy it back later for less money. Short sellers bet on, and profit from, a drop in a security's price. This can be contrasted with long investors who want the price to go up.
26. **Market Crashes** ? When the market reaches an unbelievable high, it usually results in a bubble. But because the levels are unsustainable, investors end up panicking, leading to a massive selloff. This results in a market crash.
27. **Insider Buying and Selling ?**

    insiders are the company's senior managers and directors, plus any shareholders who own at least 10% of the company's stock.3 A company's managers and directors have unique knowledge about the companies they run, so if they are purchasing its stock, it's reasonable to assume that the company's prospects look favorable.
28. **What is Scalping** ? **Scalping** is a trading strategy used by traders to make quick profits by rapidly buying and selling financial instruments such as stocks, currencies, or commodities. The goal of scalping is to take advantage of small price movements and execute multiple trades in a short period of time, typically ranging from a few seconds to a few minutes.
29. **DP in Trading** : Delivery Percentage refers to the percentage of shares that have been physically delivered to buyers as opposed to being settled through cash transactions. This can be used as an indicator of market sentiment or demand for a particular stock.
30. **Board of Directors ?** A board of directors is a group of individuals who are elected or appointed to oversee the activities of a company, organization, or non-profit entity. The board of directors is responsible

for setting strategic goals and objectives, approving major decisions and initiatives, providing guidance and advice to the executive leadership team, and ensuring that the organization is operating in compliance with legal and regulatory requirements.

31. **Promoter** ? A promoter is a person or group of people who start and establish a company or business. Promoters play a vital role in the creation of a new business as they provide the initial funding and lay the groundwork for the company's future success.
32. **Debentures ?** Debentures are a type of long-term debt security issued by companies or government entities to raise funds.

33. **Demat Account ?** A demat (short for dematerialised) account, is necessary for trading. In stock market terms this means that all of the shares, mutual funds, bonds, etc., are credited and debited through this account. A demat account can be opened by anyone through various online platforms like Zerodha, Upstox, and Delta Exchange. Certain banks also allow their customers to open a demat account.

34. Limit Order Book ? A limit order is of two types – a buy limit order and a sell limit order. A trader buys or sells a share at a preset price or higher (In case of a sell limit order) and lower (In case of a buy limit order). In stock market terms, a limit order book is simply a record of outstanding limit orders which is kept and executed by the security specialist as and when the specified price is met by the market.

35. Clearing House ? The words "clearing house" may seem straightforward in meaning, but in stock market terms it refers to an organisation which acts as a middleman between traders. After a transaction has been completed, the clearing house initiates the finalisation of the trade and ensures that both parties have been honest towards their contractual obligations. Aside from this, the clearing houses also collect margin (collateral) payments and oversee the delivery of assets.

36. Order Driven Market ? In stock market terms, an order driven market is one where both the buyers and sellers showcase their preferred buying and selling prices, as well as the number of shares they wish to deal with. It caters mainly to market and limit orders. However, there is a considerable lack of liquidity providers or market makers, and hence, liquidity.

37..Market Makers ? Market makers are either individuals or organisations which act as consultants to investors, as well as provide trading services and maintain the constant flow of the market by trading themselves. In stock market terms, this essentially means that market makers maintain the liquidity of the market by continuously buying and selling securities which they keep on behalf of their client, as and when ordered to do so.

38. Market Order ? A market order is an order which an investor or trader gives to their broker or market maker to buy and sell shares at the best possible price available in the market. In stock market terms, a market order is a price which is set by the market and not the traders.

39. Liquidity ? In stock market terms, liquidity refers to those assets which do not lose their value after being converted into cash. Assets such as gold, gems, property, etc., can be considered liquid as well, but their value as a "liquid" is less than cash.

40. Settlement Risk ? Settlement risk, while not common in trading, is still a scenario which traders should be prepared to face. In stock market terms, it is the possibility of one or both the parties failing to deliver on their end of the transaction. Settlement risk is of two types, namely, default risk and settlement timing risk. Default risk is when a trader fails to deliver entirely on the contract, even after the other party has. Settlement timing risk is less severe, as the trade still takes place, although later than the agreed-upon time period.

41.**Investment ?** Investment typically involves putting money into assets with the expectation of generating long-term returns, such as capital gains or dividend income. Investments are typically made with a view to achieving specific financial goals, such as funding retirement or paying for a child's education. The focus is on the fundamental value of the asset and its ability to generate returns over time.

42.**Speculation ?** Speculationon the other hand, involves making bets on short-term price movements of an asset, with the aim of making a quick profit. Speculators are less concerned with the fundamental value of the asset and more focused on market trends and price fluctuations. Speculation is generally considered riskier than investment because it involves making bets based on uncertain market conditions.

43. **Active investors** ? Active investors are those who aim to outperform the market by buying and selling securities frequently, often based on research and analysis of market trends and company fundamentals. Active investors often have a specific investment strategy and a targeted return on investment, and they may make frequent adjustments to their portfolio as

they identify new investment opportunities or risks.

44.**Passive investors** ? Passive investors on the other hand, aim to match the returns of the overall market or a specific index by investing in a diversified portfolio of securities and holding onto them for the long term. Passive investors do not engage in frequent buying and selling of securities and do not attempt to beat the market through individual stock selection or timing.

45.**Pre-market trading** ? Pre-market trading refers to the buying and selling of securities before the official market open, usually between 4:00 AM and 9:30 AM Eastern Time in the United States. During this time, only select exchanges are open and trading volumes tend to be lower than during regular market hours

46.**Post-market trading** ? Post-market trading on the other hand, refers to the buying and selling of securities after the official market close, usually between 4:00 PM and 8:00 PM Eastern Time in the United States. Like pre-market trading, only select exchanges are open during this time and trading volumes tend to be lower.

47.**Fixed deposits** ? Fixed deposits also known as certificates of deposit (CDs), are a type of savings account offered by banks and other financial institutions. FDs offer a fixed rate of interest over a set period of time, typically ranging from one month to several years. They are considered low-risk investments, as the principal is guaranteed and the interest rate is fixed.

48.**Bonds** ? Bonds are a type of debt instrument issued by corporations, municipalities, and governments to raise capital. When an investor buys a bond, they are essentially lending money to the issuer in exchange for a fixed rate of interest over a set period of time. Bonds are typically considered less risky than stocks because they offer fixed returns and are generally more stable.

49.**Debt equity** ? Debt equity refers to the financing of a company through borrowing (debt) and the sale of ownership stakes (equity). Debt equity financing can include loans, lines of credit, and bonds, as well as common and preferred stock. The debt portion of debt equity is typically repaid at a fixed rate of interest, while the equity portion offers investors a share of ownership in the company.

50.**Pledge and leverages ?**

A pledge is a commitment to use an asset as collateral for a loan. This means that if the borrower is unable to repay the loan, the lender has the right to seize the pledged asset and sell it to recover the amount owed.

Leverage, on the other hand, refers to the use of borrowed money to increase the potential return on an investment. By using leverage, an investor can control a larger amount of assets with a smaller amount of capital. This can increase the potential for profit, but also increases the risk of loss.

www.ingramcontent.com/pod-product-compliance
Ingram Content Group UK Ltd.
Pitfield, Milton Keynes, MK11 3LW, UK
UKHW022020190726
13853UKWH00005B/2023

9 798889 86653